Word Check 2

Over 1000 Nasty
New Problem Wo

The **One Hour Wordpower** *series*

One Hour Wordpower

Word Check 2
Over 1000 Nasty New Problem Words

GRAHAM KING

Mandarin
in association with
The Sunday Times

A Mandarin Paperback
WORD CHECK 2

First published in Great Britain 1994
by Mandarin Paperbacks
an imprint of Reed Consumer Books Ltd
Michelin House, 81 Fulham Road, London SW3 6RB
and Auckland, Melbourne, Singapore and Toronto

A CIP catalogue record for this title
is available from the British Library
ISBN 0 7493 1879 1

Printed and bound in Great Britain
by Cox & Wyman Ltd, Reading, Berkshire

Contents

Acknowledgements

The majority of the word definitions in *Word Check 2* are taken from *The Sunday Times Wordpower Dictionary* (Mandarin, 1993, paperback £3.99). Other sources for meanings and usage include the *Oxford English Dictionary* and supplements, *Collins English Dictionary*, *The Chambers Dictionary*, *Cassell's English Dictionary*, *Webster's New 20th Century Dictionary*, *Funk & Wagnalls Standard College Dictionary*, *Chambers Science and Technology Dictionary* and *The Encyclopædia Britannica*.

Acknowledgement is also made to the help supplied by H. W. Fowler's *Dictionary of Modern English Usage* (Revised by Sir Ernest Gowers), Eric Partridge's *Usage and Abusage*, the *Longman Guide to English Usage*, Sir Ernest Gowers' *The Complete Plain Words*, Stephen Murray-Smith's *Right Words*, Philip Howard's *The State of the Language*, Michael Dummett's *Grammar and Style*, Theodore Bernstein's *Miss Thistlebottom's Hobgoblins*, and the style and usage manuals of *The Sunday Times* and *The Times*.

Consultant on grammar and linguistics: Paul Coggle, Senior Lecturer in German, University of Kent in Canterbury.

Introduction

We've all heard about instant death, but is there any other kind? How can something grow smaller? Have you ever seen a self-addressed envelope? Met a criminal lawyer? Held a meeting? These are everyday expressions we read and use with hardly a thought as to what they might actually mean.

Many of us may know about Mrs Malaprop but aren't we at times all guilty of dropping the verbal brick? Using **livid** for red when it means the bluish hue of a bruise? Or vocal **chords** for vocal **cords**? **Incapable** for **unable**? And **tenderhooks** for **tenterhooks**? There are few people without some kind of mental block about certain words, which may be why an alarming percentage of the population persists in writing **a litter of cat's** and **whose this cheeky geezer**? Someone once estimated that half the population believes that any plural word ending in 's' needs an apostrophe, and that the other half either doesn't care or hardly notices.

But apostrophes apart, correct usage generally is at a pretty low ebb. The doomsters tell us that illiteracy is on the march. A recent report commissioned by the Adult Literacy and Basic Skills Unit revealed that 40% of 16 – 19-year-old students lack basic literacy and numeracy skills and according to 400 British companies this lack of basic skills is costing the UK economy some £8.4 billion a year.

But let us not get too depressed.

A national awareness of this state of affairs has inspired hundreds of thousands, perhaps millions of us – some with good educations who've gone rusty; others, less privileged and largely self-taught – to pay closer attention to our language and to hone our skill in using it. The realisation of our ability to

9

communicate with clarity, with elegance, with vivacity, is little short of magic.

But like all magic it has to be practised and this largely comes down to knowing how to use words correctly. The grammarians call it English Usage.

Flip through the pages of a dictionary. It tells you what the words mean but rarely shows you how to use them. And there, for most of us, lies the trap.

Do we write **Due to my accident** or **Owing to my accident**? In these politically correct times do we regard Jilly Cooper as an **author** or an **authoress**? Might we be **summoned** to court or **summonsed**? Do we **prise** or **pry** a jar open? Is it **Celsius** or **centrigrade**? Is **mother in law** hyphenated? If you let the hot tap run and run is it **waste** or **wastage**? Do you know – precisely – the meanings of **trauma, toothsome, tandem** and **jejune**? Have you ever used the term **actual facts**?

These are tough and gritty questions. Few of us could give all the correct answers without hesitation or running to the bookshelf.

But don't feel too bad about it. Even Dr Johnson got it wrong sometimes. Thousands of people have fun error-spotting in newspapers and magazines which, despite battalions of sub-editors combing every line, commit the grossest of solecisms.

One of life's greatest delights, however, is tripping up the experts. One classic example went the rounds in the late 1980s. A letter from a university professor appeared in an academic journal, the *American Studies International*, protesting that a previous article of his had been plagiarised. The fact that throughout the letter **plagiarise** was spelt **plagerise** rather weakened the professor's argument. The professor was, at the time, Director of Freshman English at Michigan Technological University. A tall poppy toppled by ignorance – and the English language.

Word Check 2 is not an academic tome but is designed as a welcoming, entertaining and, we hope, authoritative source of advice on a thousand or so words and expressions that are misunderstood, misused and abused.

Dive in.

Word Check 2

abjure, adjure

Not words you'd use every day but useful in
certain circumstances. **Abjure** means formally
and solemnly to renounce something, usually on
oath. **Adjure** is (equally solemnly) to charge
someone with a serious responsibility. 'He
abjured his former way of life and adjured his
family to protect him from further temptations.'

abnegate, abrogate, arrogate

This trio is often confused with the pair above.
Abnegate is to deny oneself; **abnegation** is
self-denial. To **abrogate** is to repeal or abolish
something: 'The abrogation of the despised
emergency laws was a cause for national
celebration.' **Arrogate** means to claim or seize
without right (notice the close tie with
arrogant?).

abnormal, subnormal

A significant difference here. **Abnormal** means
not normal, departing from the average,
unusual; an **abnormality** is an irregularity.
Subnormal means below normal and is often
applied to individuals to indicate a low
intelligence.

abstruse, obtuse

A concept that's **abstruse** is hard to
understand – not too dissimilar to **obscure**,
meaning unclear. **Obtuse** derives from dull and
means slow, stupid and insensitive. It is not so

much applied to concepts as people: 'The obtuseness of her pupils was never so much in evidence as it is today.'

abuse, disabuse

The range of meanings of **abuse** is well-known: to misuse, maltreat or insult. But **disabuse** has just one specific meaning which is to rid (someone) of a mistaken idea: 'She lost no time disabusing the girls of the notion that life at St Agatha's was going to be one big party.'

accede, agree

Accede, meaning to **agree** or give consent to, has become a pompous word and is now pretty much confined to legal and regal circles. Use plain **agree to, consent to** or **allow**.

accent, ascent

The word **accent** has to do with some aspect of speech and its pronunciation; **ascent** (pronounced **ass-SENT**) is the act of moving or climbing upwards.

accidental, incidental

An **accidental** happening occurs unexpectedly and unintentionally. Something **incidental** happens in relation to something else of greater importance: 'One incidental result of the calamitous floods was the *bonhomie* between neighbours who hadn't spoken to each other for years.'

accidie, anomie

Strange words that are cropping up more and more in articles and book reviews. **Accidie** (**AK-sid-dih**), or spiritual sloth, was one of the seven deadly sins; its modern meaning is the apathetic attitude of 'What's the point?' **Anomie** is the erosion or distancing of a person or a society from laws, morals and social standards. A country suffering from **anomie** is out of touch with civilised social and moral behaviour.

according to

See **pace**, according to, notwithstanding

accountable, responsible

There seems to be no good reason to regard both words other than as synonyms. Gowers views **accountable** as voguish. See also **cause, responsible**.

Actor, actress, authoress, poetess, sculptress

Actor was used for both sexes before the introduction of **actress** and today there is a general return to the former with its non-feminine suffix. Fair enough: there is no Actress's Equity in the UK nor a Screen Actress's Guild in the US. But while we don't differentiate between male and female artists, we do with **authoress, poetess, sculptress** and a host of others. Feminists have strenuously lobbied against these labels as perpetuating the idea that the male form is the norm and the female a secondary or inferior subset. It is true that sometimes feminine qualifications are used pejoratively, but to insist that **hero** should replace **heroine**, **heir** replace **heiress**, **waiter** replace **waitress** and for **god** to replace **goddess** is perhaps going too far.

15

acquire

See **get, acquire, obtain, secure**

adapt, adopt

To **adapt** means to change or adjust something to suit different conditions; to **adopt** is to take over something or someone as one's own. 'In time they adapted their eating habits to the tropical climate'; 'Once he understood what it was about he adopted the idea with enthusiasm.'

adjacent, adjoining, contiguous

If two things are **adjacent** they are close to each other. If they are **adjoining**, they are actually joined or touching: 'My room adjoins hers; Marie's house is adjacent.' **Contiguous** means sharing a common boundary.

adjudge, adjudicate

To **adjudge** is to decide but usually to decide judicially in a court of law. To **adjudicate** is a serious, although less formal, process of giving a decision.

adjure

See **abjure, adjure**

admit

There is nothing wrong with 'Alleged thief admits four robberies in West London.' But what we are increasingly seeing is 'Customs Officer admits to filing false claims'. If you substituted **acknowledges** for **admits**, would you write **acknowledges to**? In this sense the **to** after **admits** is redundant.

administer, minister

In the sense of **treating** and **tending to** both
words have similar meanings but are used
differently. 'The nurse administered what
emergency first aid she could'; 'Over the course
of the next few months she patiently ministered
to their medical needs.' Note that in this
context, **minister** is always followed by **to**
(unlike **admit**, above).

adventitious, adventurous

In the synonym stakes, **adventitious** has all but
given way to **fortuitous** and **serendipitous**; they
all mean happening by sheer chance.
Adventurous means daring, enterprising, bold
and audacious.

advice, advise, advisedly

No problems with the first two; if you give
counsel to or **advise** someone you are giving them
information or **advice**. **Advisedly** is the trick
card – it has nothing to do with being advised
or receiving advice. It means to take your own
counsel with full consideration and forethought.
In a looser sense it can mean **prudently**,
discreetly and **cautiously**: 'The King made
the decision, advisedly, no doubt with the aim of
dividing the troublesome clans.'

aesthetic, ascetic, acetic

Aesthetic relates to the appreciation of beauty
in art and nature above material considerations;
an **aesthete** is one who has a highly developed
appreciation for artistic beauty. An **ascetic** is a
person who rejects worldly comforts in favour of
self-denial, often for religious reasons. **Acetic**,
from acetic acid, the main component of vinegar,

is sometimes used as an adjective for sour and bitter. Pronunciations of these three words are **es-THET-ik, ah-SET-ik, ah-SEE-tik**.

affront, effrontery

These are easily confused but are used in different ways. An **affront** is a deliberate, contemptuous insult. **Effrontery** means barefaced insolence, high-handed impudence: 'The effrontery of the performers was an affront to every decent family there.'

Agenda and other problem plurals

'The agenda were agreed by all present'; 'In the light of the findings the original data were reviewed'; 'She agreed reluctantly that her criteria for the investigation were at fault.' These sentences may sound strange but technically, perhaps pedantically, they are all correct. The fact is that we have abandoned many singular forms of Greek- and Latin-derived words. **Agenda** was the plural of **agendum**, but today we use **agenda** as the singular word and **agendas** as the plural. **Datum**, the singular form of **data**, has also slipped from use, and **data** now serves for both singular and plural. **Erotica** is plural, but did you ever come across the singular? (It exists only in the original Greek, *erotikos*.) **Trivia** is another tricky one, existing only in the plural.

Here, for the record, are the most common 'lost singulars':

ago, before, back, past

Most dictionaries define **ago** as 'in the past', so it is correct to write: 'The O'Briens left these shores over a century ago.' In such a context **ago** is preferable to the other choices: 'a century before' and 'a century past' beg the question, 'before or past what?'; while 'a century back' is idiomatic. A common mistake is to couple **ago** with **since**: 'It was over a century ago since the O'Brien's left', where since is clearly redundant. The correct version would be: 'It was over a century ago that the O'Brien's left.' Or, without **ago**: 'It was over a century since the O'Briens left.'

SINGULAR	PLURAL
datum	data
stratum	strata
phenomenon	phenomena
criterion	criteria
–	trivia
medium	media
minutia	minutiae
–	erotica
bacterium	bacteria
species	species
spectrum	spectra
graffito	graffiti

Don't get caught out on **kudos**, however; it is singular, pure and simple. And while you're thinking about all this, are words like **acoustics** and **politics** singular or plural? (They are both plural nouns functioning as singular.)

aid, abet, aid and abet

Both **aid** and **abet** have a common meaning which is to assist, help or encourage. **Abet** is now virtually confined to police circles while **aid and abet** is nothing but legal tautology.

AIDS, HIV

AIDS is the acronym for Acquired Immune Deficiency Syndrome, and is a medical condition, not a disease; strictly speaking you cannot die of **AIDS**. However, people who are **HIV** (human immunodeficiency virus) **positive** may die of **AIDS**-related diseases.

alibi, excuse

Increasingly, **alibi** is being used as a synonym for **excuse**, to the extent that Fowler worries that we shall be left with no word for the true meaning of **alibi**. 'The Government is using French intransigence as an alibi for its own slow progress on free trade agreements' is wrong. An **alibi** is the defence that an accused person could not have committed a crime because he or she was elsewhere at the time. Ignore dictionaries that suggest **excuse** as an informal meaning of **alibi**; **excuses** are explanations to cover some fault or shortcoming; they can be true or false and come in a thousand guises.

allegory, fable, myth, parable, legend

An **allegory** is a play, poem or picture in which the characters symbolise a deeper moral message. A **fable** is a short story, usually improbable, usually with a moral, and usually with animals as characters. A **parable** is a short and simple story which illustrates some religious or moral principle. The original **myths** used ancient gods and superhuman characters to explain natural phenomena and social customs; today the word is used mostly to describe a baseless popular belief. A **legend** is a traditional story, popularly thought to be true or based on fact: the Arthurian legends are an example. But the word is now extensively used to describe an enduring feat or someone whose notoriety has spread and persisted, e.g. 'the legendary cricketer W. C. Grace', – even though Grace did exist in fact. The cliché 'He was a legend in his lifetime' is surely an oxymoron.

allergy, aversion

An **allergy** is any oversensitive reaction by the body to some substance; hay fever is an **allergic** reaction to pollen. But **allergy** is not a synonymn for **aversion**. We often read: 'The man is allergic to any form of hard work', whereas what is meant is: 'The man has an aversion for any form of hard work.'

all is not well, not all is well

If you use this cliché, as in: '**All is not well** at the Framlington Brewery this week', it may pay you to pause and think about what you really mean. If you mean that all – everything – at the brewery is ailing and in a bad way, well and good. But if you mean to convey merely that something or some aspects of the brewery are amiss, then you should use **not all is well**, or abandon the cliché altogether.

all ready, already

All ready, meaning prepared and ready for an eventuality, is clear enough, but **already** presents problems. **Already** means by a certain time, or before a specified time. Follow? Precisely. Sentences like: 'You want me to leave already?' do have a certain Yiddish flavour, but are acceptable. So are expressions like: 'We're already in plenty of trouble'; 'I've already done it'; 'The deliveries are already running late.' **Already** is a sort of all-purpose word which vaguely expresses a time relationship, and its use is becoming increasingly idiomatic.

Ambition vs policy

If there is a tendency to use the word **policy** where **ambition** would be the correct term then journalist Peter Barnard is doing a sterling job trying to halt it. Here he is in *The Times* berating Prime Minister John Major:

'Whereas Major used to give the impression that he did not know the answer to some questions, he is now obliged . . . to give the impression that there is nothing for which he does not have a solution.

'This sad development involves speaking when silence would be better, and in speaking, abusing the English language. Thus we have Major saying that the government has a policy called low inflation. Low inflation is not a policy, it is an ambition. As a young man I wanted to sleep with Catherine Deneuve, but this was an ambition, not a policy. Low inflation is Major's Catherine Deneuve.'

allude, elude

Allude means to refer to something indirectly; **elude** (think of elusive) means to escape by cunning or skill.

ambiguous, ambivalent

The two are not synonyms. **Ambiguous** is used to refer to a situation which has two or more meanings or interpretations. **Ambivalent** is really a psycho-analytical definition of a mind that experiences contradictory thoughts and emotions at the same time; careful writers will use it only in that context.

ameliorate

See **improve, ameliorate**

amend, emend

In relation to a text, **amend** means to improve, change or revise it, while **emend** means to correct it and make it free from errors. **Amend** is nowadays acceptable for both tasks.

angry

See **mad, angry**

anomie

See **accidie, anomie**

anniversary, birthday

A small point, perhaps, but humans and animals celebrate their birth with **birthdays** while everything else has **anniversaries**.

antagonist

See **protagonist, antagonist**

ante-, anti-

When using words beginning with these prefixes
it may help to remember that **ante = before**;
anti = against:

- **antenatal, antebellum, antedate,
  antecedent**
- **antifreeze, antibody, antimacassar,
  antinuclear**

anyplace, anywhere

Anywhere means any unspecified place. So does
anyplace, but only in the US and Canada.

apposite, apt

Both mean appropriate or ideal to the occasion
or purpose. **Apposite** perhaps carries a little
literary weight, that's all.

apartment

See **flat, condominium, apartment**

appreciate

See **understand, appreciate, comprehend**

approve

See **condone, approve, allow**

a priori, prima facie

The term *a priori*, which is sometimes
misapplied, defines deductive reasoning, from
cause to effect, which without supportive
observation leads to a conclusion. **A priori**
reasoning can, of course, lead to a wrong
conclusion. **A priori** is sometimes confused
with **prima facie**, which means using available
but not necessarily complete or tested evidence

to arrive at a conclusion.

arbitrate, mediate

These words represent quite distinct methods of settling a dispute. An **arbitrator** hears evidence from both sides before handing down a decision, which is binding; an **arbitrary decision** is one over which the disputants have little or no say. A **mediator** is much more involved in negotiating with the parties and aims more for a compromise solution.

Argentina, Argentine

Argentina is the country, whose citizens are **Argentinian**. **Argentine** is an adjective, as in: 'Argentine beef is still considered the best.' Expect arguments, however; old hands still refer to **The Argentine** and **Argentines**.

around

See **round, around, about**

arouse

See **rouse, arouse**

artist, artiste

A painter or public performer is an **artist,** and although the inflated **artiste** still survives, it is best avoided.

ascent

See **accent, ascent**

ascertain, find out

'Jim, find out how many people are out there, will you?'; 'Jim, ascertain how many people are out there, will you?' There's little doubt that the phrasal verb **find out** wins every time. But if you can substitute **ascertain** without appearing pompous, by all means do so.

ascetic
See **aesthetic, ascetic, acetic**

ascribe
See **prescribe, ascribe**

astronaut, cosmonaut
American space travellers are **astronauts**; the Russians have **cosmonauts**. Why? The Americans plumped for the Latin *astrum*, which means star (although the Greek *astro* also translates as star), while the Russians, with their Greek-derived Cyrillic alphabet, took their cue from *Kosmos*, or universe. It is likely that **astronaut** will prevail.

at your convenience, soon
Dump the first and replace with shorter and more specific directions: **soon, promptly, shortly, immediately, speedily, without delay, in reasonable time**.

auger, augur
Bill Bryson quotes the *Guardian* as saying, 'The results do not auger well for the President in the forthcoming mid-term elections.' What the *Guardian* is saying is that 'the results do not drill well for the President'. An **auger** is a large boring tool. **Augur** means forsee, presage, indicate; 'do not bode well' would be a suitable substitute.

authoritarian, authoritative

An **authoritarian** rules by fear, demanding obedience. An **authoritative** person commands respect because of his or her mastery of some aspect of learning.

aversion

See **allergy, aversion**

avocation

See **vocation, avocation**

await, wait

The two forms are used differently though in the end they amount to much the same thing. We **await** the judge's decision; we **await** news of the survivors. In other words, one awaits something. But, 'We **wait for** the judge's decision'; 'We **wait to** hear about the survivors'; 'We **wait until** early morning for the news.' **Await**, it must be said, is heading towards obsolescence.

back

See **ago, before, back, past**

bail, bale

The fairly wide acceptance of interchangeable spellings has only added to the confusion that these two words have always caused. **Bail**, the money paid by a person to release someone charged by a court of law and forfeited if that person absconds, is fairly straightforward. So is a **bale** of hay, wool, paper or other such bundle. But do you **bale out** or **bail out** the water in a swamped dinghy? If you respect the Old French origin of bucket – *baille* – you will use **bail**; otherwise either will do. More perplexing is whether you **bale out** or **bail out** of a doomed aircraft; or whether you **bale** or **bail** someone out of trouble. Here either spelling is also acceptable. The two wooden spindles placed on top of cricket stumps are spelt **bails**; the mystery is, why?

baleful, baneful

Baleful is occasionally used incorrectly to mean **miserable** and **dejected**, but that meaning expired a century or more ago. Its modern meaning is menacing, malign or destructive. **Baneful** is little used today, but means poisonous or harmful.

base, basis

Although **base** has a wide range of meanings, in the sense of defining a foundation, a support or a fundamental element in a structure, both **base** and **basis** mean the same. They are, however, used differently. **Base** is usually applied to literal description (**base** of a pyramid, a skull, a compound) while **basis** finds more figurative or abstract uses (**basis** of an agreement, **basis** of a solution etc).

base, bass

Whatever confusion there is here probably derives from the fact that the musical **bass** (voice range, instrument) is pronounced **bayss**.

bathos, pathos, bathetic, pathetic

Apart from its precise meaning of an undignified descent from the sublime to the commonplace, **bathos** is also loosely used to convey pompous insincerity, excessive sentimentality and a really low point – the pits. **Pathos** is the quality of drama to arouse deep feelings of pity and compassion. The adjectives **pathetic** and **bathetic**, however, are today often contemptuously used to indicate utter worthlessness, so be careful.

belabour, labour

Occasionally **belaboured** is used as a synonym for **laboured**, which it isn't. **Belabour** can mean physically to beat someone or something, or to pound verbally: 'He belaboured his opponent with his sorry political record.'

bell-wether, harbinger

Increasingly seen in the financial pages of newspapers, **bell-wether** is the word frequently used wrongly in place of a **harbinger**, which is someone or something that foretells of an approaching event. A **bell-wether** was tradition-ally a sheep with a bell hanging from its neck which was used to lead the flock. The modern meaning is therefore something which others follow blindly, like sheep: 'The share issue proved to be a mesmerising bell-wether which predictably resulted in the usual sacrificial slaughter.'

bereft, bereaved

Both words have the common meaning of **deprived**, but while **bereft** is used generally – 'She was suddenly and tragically bereft of sustenance, of hope, of all human dignity' – **bereaved** is reserved for deprivation by death.

birthday

See **anniversary, birthday**

blanch, blench

Strange word, **blanch**. Although in cook-books it can mean plunging vegetables into boiling water to preserve their colour, it usually means to remove colour, to lighten or whiten. Thus, if someone received a shock he or she might **blanch** or go pale: 'She shuddered, and blanched at the thought.' **Blench** is also a strange one; from an older meaning of 'to deceive' it now means to 'flinch from in fear'. Many dictionaries unhelpfully list both meanings under both words. Final warning: do not confuse **blench** with **belch**.

blaze, blazon

Apart from its use to describe fire and light, **to blaze** means to mark or open up a path or territory: 'He blazed a new trail into California.' Occasionally we see the word **blazoned** wrongly substituted for **blazed**. To **blazon** means to proclaim something loudly to all and sundry and, in heraldry, to draw up heraldic arms.

blench

See **blanch, blench**

bloc, block

When do you use **bloc** instead of **block**? When you are describing a group of individuals, organisations or nations united in a common cause. The best-known example was probably the Soviet bloc.

boar, boor, bore, Boer

Although a dictionary soon sorts them out, this quartet is commonly confused, misspelled, and, these days, usually pronounced the same. A **boar** is a male pig; a **boor** is a rude, insensitive, uncivilised person; a **bore** is a garrulous, tiresome and fiendishly uninteresting person from whose clutches one can't wait to escape; and the **Boers** were the original white, mostly Dutch, settlers in South Africa.

bogey, bogie, bogy

A **bogey** in golf is par or a score of one stroke over par for a particular hole on a course. A **bogie** is the set of wheels, usually four or six, on locomotives or at either end of railway carriages; a **bogy** (as in bogyman) is an evil spirit and also something unmentionable from the nose.

bona fide, bona fides

Bona fide, which looks like the singular of **bona fides**, actually isn't. It's the adjectival form: 'He judged it to be a bona fide complaint', meaning a genuine one. **Bona fides** is the noun and it is singular, so be careful to use it in the singular sense: 'He hoped his bona fides was sufficiently convincing to allow him entry.'

burglar, burgle, burglarise

A **burglar** breaks into premises to steal, or to **burgle**. **Burglarise**, from the US, is now considered to be a respectable substitute for **burgle**.

bursar

See **registrar, bursar, bursary**

bust, burst

Do you **bust** a balloon, or **burst** it? Careful users will **burst** a balloon and use **bust** only in informal contexts: 'The firm went bust'; 'The night-club is busted at least twice a year'; 'It was quite a bust-up.'

Broken up, broken down and other phrasal verbs

Take a typical verb: **break**. Its primary meaning is to separate, or damage. Now see how, by simply tacking on a adverb or preposition, we can create a string of new meanings:

break down, break with, break in, break out, break off, break through, break up, break away from

These are known as phrasal verbs, and we use them constantly:

turn off, turn up, turn down, turn out; give in, give up, give back; look out, look after, look up, look over, look back, look forward to . . . there are thousands of these versatile verbs and life would be difficult without them.

The trouble is, we like them so much we invent ones which are quite meaningless. Take, for example, **slow down** and **slow up; down** and **up** add nothing to the original meaning of **slow** but the expressions are now so ingrained in the language as to be irremovable. Others include **check out, eat up, sell off, cut back, phone up,** and **meet with**.

cache, cachet

A **cache** is a hidden store of treasure, documents, food, etc.; a **cachet** is a stamp or seal of approval. The pronunciations are **kash** and **kah-SHAY**.

candelabra, chandelier

These two words are sometimes confused. **Candelabra** (the singular = **candelabrum**) are branched candle holders; a **chandelier** is an ornamental hanging light.

canvas, canvass

Canvas is a heavy cloth; **to canvass** is to solicit – votes, opinions or sales orders. But note: 'His collection included twenty canvasses by Bacon'; 'He regularly canvasses the Brighton area.'

capsize

The British book and newspaper industries today prefer the **-ise** suffix to **-ize**: **regularise, supervise, personalise, privatise**. One exception is, of course, **capsize**.

cardinal

See **crucial, cardinal**

carousal, carousel

A **carousal** is a boisterous, well-lubricated drinking party; a **carousel** is a fairground merry-go-round and also that revolving conveyer at airports on which you vainly search for your luggage. They are pronounced **kuh-ROW-suhl** and **kar-ruh-SEL**.

cash

See **money, monies, funds, cash**

caster, castor

In terms of edibility these should not be confused for good reasons. **Caster** is very finely ground sugar, a sweetener; **castor** oil is a purgative. The swivelling little wheels on the legs of furniture can be spelt as either **casters** or **castors**.

casual, causal

Casual means happening by chance, informal or unconcerned; **causal** relates or refers to a cause: 'Theirs was merely a brief, casual affair'; 'The causal agent for the environmental damage was undoubtedly the build-up of nitrates.'

Catachrestically speaking . . .

One of the pet hates of novelist Kingsley Amis is, perhaps unsurprisingly, **catachresis**, or the incorrect use of words – which is, of course, what the *Word Check* books are all about. Any dictionary that misguidedly allows the admission of new meanings to a word that renders it ambiguous becomes the object of Amis's wrath, a fearsome spectacle indeed.

Some of the catachreses Amis particularly deplores include:

aggravate to mean irritate; **epithet** to mean a term of abuse; **crescendo** to mean climax; **dilemma** to mean a problem; **fulsome** to mean lavish; **pristine** to mean clean (a common misconception); **brutalise** to mean maltreat; **infamous** to mean quaint; **peremptory** to mean sudden; **quixotic** to mean absurb and **schizophrenic** to mean divided.

---

cause, responsible

Thick fog is not **responsible** for motorway pile-ups; a violent storm is not **responsible** for death and damage. Things can **cause** pile-ups, death and damage but only people bear **responsibility** for their actions.

ceiling, maximum

Ceiling is a figurative term used to express a limit or maximum but it is often used incorrectly, as in: 'The committee agreed that, under the circumstances, the ceiling would be appropriately increased.' A **ceiling**, if you think

The correct or currently accepted meanings of most of these and scores more catachreses will be found in this book and its companion, the first *Word Check* volume. At the same time allowance must be made for changes in meaning over a length of time. Whether we or Mr Amis like it or not, alternative meanings of words must at least be recognised through sheer weight of usage; **pristine** to mean 'perfect' or 'perfectly clean' is an example. Another example is **consummate** which Mr Amis would today no doubt correctly use in the sense of 'to make complete, or to bring to perfection'. Yet during this century consummate was one of his hated catachreses; its primary meaning, as typically recorded in the 1901 *Chambers' Twentieth Century Dictionary*, was 'to raise to the highest point'.

about it, can be raised or lowered but not increased.

Celsius, centigrade
See **centigrade, Celsius**

censer, censor, censure
A **censer** is the container in which incense is
burned during religious ceremonies. A **censor**
is a person who, usually by authority, suppresses
matter – written, drawn or otherwise
expressed – on moral or political grounds. To
censure is to reprimand severely.

centering, centring
Centering means to place in the centre;
centring is a temporary structure used to
support an archway during construction.

centigrade, Celsius
The Swede, Anders Celsius, invented
centigrade, a temperature guage, which sets 0
degrees as freezing point and 100 degrees as
boiling point. Both terms mean the same.

chafe, chaff
To **chafe** is to irritate or make sore by rubbing;
to **chaff** is to tease light-heartedly.

chaotic, inchoate
These two are wonderful confusables. **Chaotic**
needs little explanation: totally disordered,
confused and seemingly out of control.
Inchoate, perhaps because in appearance it sits
somewhere between **incoherent** and **chaotic**,
appears to be related to those words, but it isn't.
It means 'just beginning', undeveloped,

incomplete: 'The inchoate nature of the plans made it difficult for the committee to visualise the sculptor's ambitious project.'

character
See **trait, character**

chary
See **wary, chary**

chemist, druggist, pharmacist
The **chemist** most familiar to us is a **pharmacist**, who is qualified to prepare and dispense drugs and medicines. But there are countless varieties of **chemists**: agricultural, analytical, organic, inorganic, molecular, to name just a few. A pharmacist in North America is called a **druggist**.

choose, pick
These are synonymous, **pick** being the more idiomatic, as in 'take your pick'. 'Make a **choice**' here would be considered more elegant.

chords, cords
The confusion between these two arises from **chords**, the group of musical notes, when applied to the voice. 'It was feared that Miss Caparello's vocal chords were damaged in the accident' is incorrect: what were damaged were her vocal **cords**.

chutney
See **ketchup, sauce, chutney**

cite
See **quote, cite**

classic, classical

While **classical** largely retains its original meaning, which is relating to the ancient Greek and Roman civilisations, **classic** has become a grab-bag of moveable meanings. We often hear the phrase 'It's a classic!' What does it mean? Traditionally it has been used to describe the highest achievements in literature and the arts. This has spilled over into other areas of achievement: classic cars, classic stamps, classic horse races, classic fashion, classic jazz and so on. There's nothing wrong with describing something that's excellent as a 'classic of its kind', but this useful word should not be carelessly devalued.

climb down

'Inch by heart-stopping inch he climbed down the treacherous ravine.' Isn't there a contradiction here? Those who respect the meaning of **climb** as 'to ascend' may prefer 'he descended into the ravine'. But the term is now ingrained and a second meaning has been acquired which is to 'retreat from a position'. **Climb up** is redundant; **climb** is all you need.

collaborate, cooperate

To **collaborate** is to work jointly with someone, usually on some specific project. To **cooperate** (or **co-operate**) is to work with someone or be willing to help or contribute: 'The two scientists had always cooperated with each other, and had collaborated on several research programmes.' Curiously, if you **cooperate** with the enemy you are a **collaborator**.

collectable, collectible

Usage is fairly divided. Until recently
collectible had the ascendancy, but now, with
Sotheby's and Christie's auction houses, and
thus top people, using **collectable**, the former
may suffer a setback.

collision, collusion

A **collision** is the impact of two moving objects
or forces; a **collusion** is a conspiracy to deceive.
'They were forever colluding against the rightful
owners of the land.'

comic, comical

Comic is something that is intended to be funny;
a **comical** situation may be hilarious but
unintentional. Where tragedy, real or theatrical,
is shared with the humour, the same principle
applies: **tragicomic** and **tragicomical**.

commensurate, consummate

Commensurate means corresponding or
roughly proportionate in size, amount or
degree: 'The guidelines he laid down were
commensurate with the laws of the previous
administration.' **Consummate** has two
meanings: 'Highly skilled and accomplished';
and 'to complete': 'With consummate ease and
considerable enthusiasm the pair consummated
their marriage between Innsbruck and Venice on
the Orient Express.'

Common Market

See **European Union, European Community,
Common Market**

compatriot
See **expatriate, compatriot**

compel, impel
The interesting difference between these two is
that if you are **compelled** to do something it
is because of some outside force or pressure that
you can't resist, and over which you have little
or no control. But if you are **impelled** to do
something, the decision is yours, despite the
pressure, the urging and all the reasons.

complacent, complaisant
Spelt differently, pronounced the same, and
closely related in meaning. A **complacent**
person is self-satisfied, placid, even smug; a
complaisant person is always rather eager to
please others and will do anything to oblige.

completion
See **fruition, completion**

comprehend
See **understand, appreciate, comprehend**

compulsive, compulsory
Compulsory means obligatory, by law,
regulation or some other force. **Compulsive**
means being subject to some degree of
compulsion, either mental, moral or physical.
'Ray was a compulsive gambler'; 'The new
television crime series is compulsive viewing.'
In both cases there is an implication of addiction
or inability to resist.

condominium
See **flat, condominium, apartment**

Condone, approve, allow

In her bestselling book on sex, *The Hite Report*, the American author Shere Hite tapped out a common misconception: 'Heterosexual intercourse . . . is the only form of sexual pleasure really condoned in our society.' It is doubtful if Ms Hite meant that heterosexual intercourse was overlooked or forgiven or excused, for that is what **condone** means although it is commonly used as a substitute for **allowed** or **approved**. It is also incorrectly used in the negative sense as a synonym for disapproval: 'My position is that I neither condone nor condemn fox hunting.'

confident
See **optimistic, confident**

confident, confidant
To be **confident** is to be assured, sure of yourself, without doubts. A **confidant** (**kon-fih-DANT**) is a trusted friend to whom you confide your closest secrets. If the friend is female, use the feminine **confidante**.

congenial
See **genial, congenial, congenital**

conjugal, connubial
These are virtual synonyms. Because its most frequent usage is in the phrase 'conjugal rights', **conjugal** seems to relate more to the responsibilities of marriage, while **connubial** ('connubial bliss') hints at the joys of the union.

constraint, restraint

Both are forms of restriction but one is often self-imposed and the other originates from outside forces. A **constraint** is something that prevents a person pursuing some action: 'Her aristocratic breeding acted as a constraint to her speaking freely.' **Restraint** is self-control, the ability to check or moderate one's actions, passions or impulses.

contemptuous, contemptible

To be **contemptuous** means to be scornful, arrogant, sneering and insulting. The object of this scorn could very well be **contemptible** and deserving of contempt: 'You, sir, are nothing but a comtemptible scoundrel!'

contiguous

See **adjacent, adjoining, contiguous**

coral, corral

Coral consists of the skeletons of marine creatures which form reefs; a **corral** is an enclosure for horses or cattle.

corps, corpse, copse

A seemingly simple trio but people do confuse them. A **corps** (pronounced **kor**) consists of two or more army divisions; a **corpse** is of course a dead body; a **copse** is a thicket of trees or bushes.

cosmetic

See **superficial, cosmetic**

cosmonaut

See **astronaut, cosmonaut**

counterpoint
See **melodical mischief-makers**

Couple, two

A **couple** is, as everyone knows, two people, or a pair. **Couple** looks like and seems like a collective noun, and should therefore be singular: 'The couple with the display of roses was judged to be the winners of the section.' Fair enough. But: 'The young couple was injured when their motorcycle hit the kerb and ran out of control.' Trouble there. And: 'Mr Cartwright told the judge that the couple had separated and was living separately.' Both these cases require **couple** to be treated as a plural noun. Although **couple** theoretically functions as singular or plural, the pluralists are clearly winning.

---

covert, overt

Covert means concealed, secret, disguised; **overt** is the opposite – open to view, public and free for all to see.

crapulous

In a review of a biography of the poet Dylan Thomas and his wife Caitlin, the reviewer regarded the tone of much of the account as 'crapulous'. This was not meant as an insult to the biographer. Those familiar with the fact that the couple were (note the plural, see above) ferocious drinkers for most of their lives would have had a clue: **crapulous** means given to extreme intemperance.

crass, silly, stupid, gross

Of these terms of abuse, **silly** is the mildest, with **stupid** close behind. Both are often applied to oneself, but one would be unlikely to label oneself as **crass** or **gross**. To be **crass** is to be extremely thick, ignorant and insensitive. **Gross** is all of these with an overlay of repulsiveness, coarseness and vulgarity. Reserve it for someone special.

credible, creditable, credulous

Credible means believeable; **creditable** means deserving credit or praise; **credulous** means a naïve readiness to believe in something.

crotch, crutch, crux

One of the more hilarious malapropisms on record is, 'I'm not going to rest until I get to the crutch of the matter.' The word intended, of course, was **crux**, meaning the essential or fundamental point [of a problem or puzzle]. The **crotch** is the genital area of the human body and also, in tailoring, the inner join of the legs of a pair of trousers. **Crutch** is also sometimes used in this sense but more correctly defines a support, its original meaning.

crucial, cardinal

If something is **crucial** it is critically decisive: 'There is no doubt that O'Brien's brilliant tackling will be crucial to our winning the match.' If something is **cardinal**, it is fundamental: 'The coach claimed that O'Brien's inclusion in the team was of cardinal importance if it was to win.' And remember the **cardinal virtues**: justice, prudence, temperance and fortitude.

cultured, cultivated

In the sense of refined, educated, exhibiting good taste, these words are now accepted as synonyms.

Cyprus, cypress

Cyprus is the former British colony, now a split republic situated in the Mediterranean; a **cypress** is a coniferous tree.

debate

'Howe will debate Thatcher' is incorrect usage. You may **have a debate**, be **engaged in a debate**, or **debate a subject**: 'Howe will debate "government during the 1980s" with former Prime Minister Thatcher.'

decry, descry

To **decry** is to disparage or condemn; to **descry** something is to detect or discover it by careful looking.

deduce, deduct, adduce

The confusion between the first two probably arises from the fact that their nouns are spelt the same – **deduction**. But **deduce** means to arrive at a conclusion by reasoning; while **deduct** means to subtract or take away. To **adduce** is to present something as an example of evidence or proof: 'The hypnotist adduced a series of demonstrations, to the amusement of the audience.'

defective, deficient

There is a quality/quantity difference between these two. **Defective** means that something is faulty; **deficient** means that something is missing.

defer, delay

There is a subtle difference here for those who value finesse. **Defer** implies a decision to postpone, while **delay** carries with it overtones of slowing up a process, hindering and procrastination: 'The final decision was deferred until January'; 'The difficulties with the new computer network is delaying completion of the new production line.'

deleterious, harmful

These are synonymous and the trend is to use the simpler, better understood **harmful**.

denigration, denegation

Denigration is the disparaging or belittling of someone; **denegation** is a denial or refusal of a request.

deplete

See **exhaust, deplete, reduce**

depository, repository

Although somewhat interchangeable, a **depository** is more correctly a warehouse used for storage, while a **repository** is generally some place of indeterminate size used for storing or displaying things. A chest can be a repository for shoes; 'Leonardo's notebook was the repository of many of the world's most brilliant ideas'; 'The British Museum is one of the greatest repositories of Egyptian artifacts in the world.'

derby, Derby

A **derby** is a bowler hat; **Derby** is the capital of Derbyshire in England; a variety of cheese; and the classic annual horse race held at Epsom Downs in Surrey. Both are pronounced **DARbee**.

deserts, desserts

Surprisingly, these are commonly confused. Note the correct spelling of the word in the well-known phrase, 'He got his just deserts', meaning 'he got what he deserved'. A **desert** is an arid, usually sandy region; **dessert** is the sweet course of a meal.

detract, distract

To **detract** is to take away from, or diminish: 'Her rudeness detracted from the otherwise good impression we'd had of her.' To **distract** is to divert someone's attention away from what they're doing: 'It is unlawful to distract the driver while the vehicle is in motion.'

device, devise

Device is a noun, and is a contrivance or creation intended for a specific purpose: 'The electric potato peeler was one of the most intriguing devices she'd ever seen.' **Devise** is a verb: 'The inventor had spent three years devising the electric potato peeler.'

diametric, opposite, opposed

Many of us use the terms **diametrically opposed** and **diametrically opposite** without knowing quite what they mean. **Diametrically** means completely, directly and irreconcilably opposite, so the terms are redundancies and also clichés. Wary users will simply use **opposite** or **opposed,** or alternative clichés such as **violently opposed**.

different
See **disparate, different**

dilate, dilatory
To **dilate** something is to expand it; to be **dilatory** is to waste time.

directly
The traditional meaning of **directly** is immediately, at once: 'She went to him directly she entered the room.' But a confusing secondary meaning is entering the scene, meaning soon, in a short while, when I'm ready: 'Arthur shouted that he'd be down directly, and went on with his meal.' Avoid confusion by sticking with the original usage. See also **soon, presently**.

disabuse
See **abuse, disabuse**

discomfit, discomfort, discomfiture
Discomfort means, as the word suggests, lack of comfort; pain, distress. To **discomfit** someone is to disconcert, frustrate or embarrass them. **Discomfiture** is the noun: 'There was national sympathy for the miners, who were obviously enjoying the discomfiture of the owners.' There is no such word as **discomforture**.

disparate, different

Different means not the same; completely or partly unlike something else. **Disparate** means utterly different, with nothing whatsoever in common.

disparity, discrepancy

Both of these words indicate a 'difference'. **Disparity** highlights some inequality: 'The disparity between the wages of men and women at the plant was hard to defend.' A **discrepancy** is a difference that shouldn't exist at all: 'The investigators soon uncovered the glaring discrepancies in the company's recent annual reports.'

dissatisfied, unsatisfied

To be **dissatisfied** is to be discontented, displeased, unhappy, disappointed. To be **unsatisfied** is to feel the lack or want of something: 'Apart from his dissatisfaction with the menu, the minuscule portions ensured that he left the table quite unsatisfied.'

dissemble, disassemble

Confusingly, the opposite of **assemble** is not **dissemble** but **disassemble**: 'The entire machine could be assembled and disassembled in less than a day.' **Dissemble** means to conceal by pretence: 'His evil intentions were dissembled by a pious demeanour.'

dissociate, disassociate

Quite contrary to the previous entry, not only is **dissociate** the opposite to **associate**, but so is **disassociate**! Take your choice, but **dissociate** is less of a mouthful.

distinguish, differentiate

In the sense of detecting the difference between things the two are synonymous, but **differentiate** has an added shade of meaning which is to discriminate: 'The assistant then proceeded to differentiate between the genetic clusters using a code of coloured dyes.'

distract

See **detract**, **distract**

distrust, mistrust

To **distrust** someone is to suspect strongly that he or she is dishonest or untrustworthy. To **mistrust** is to have doubts, to be wary or sceptical. You can **mistrust** (not **distrust**) your own feelings and judgement at times.

divers, diverse

Divers is an old-fashioned word which is little used now, meaning several, various, sundry. **Diverse** means varied, assorted, of many and different kinds: 'We will never cease to be astounded by the diverse creatures of the sea.' Or to use the noun form: 'We will never cease to be astounded by the diversity of the creatures of the sea.'

Domesday, doomsday

The *Domesday Book* is the survey of England made in 1086; **doomsday** is the biblical day of judgement.

dominate, domineer

To **dominate** is to control or rule over; to **domineer** is to tyrannise.

donate, give

In his *The Complete Plain Words*, Sir Ernest Gowers advises succinctly: 'Use give.' However, in the context of giving money or time to charity or organs to medical science, **donate** is well understood.

Draught, draughts, draughtsman, draftsman

Draught is an English survivor. In the US even the game of **draughts** is called **checkers** and otherwise the spelling **draft** is used. In British English the following differences are preserved:

draught: A current of air; a quantity of liquid; a dose of medicine; beer on draught; the depth of a loaded boat; a draught-horse; draughting a plan or map.
draft: To compose a preliminary outline of a book or speech; to draw up a parliamentary bill; a banker's order for payment; to separate, usually sheep or cattle.

A person who draws maps and plans is a **draughtsman** (or, if you wish, **draughtswoman**); the official who draws up parliamentary bills is the government **draftsman**.

---

doubtless, undoubtedly

By comparison with the more forceful and unequivocal **undoubtedly**, **doubtless** is rather passive, but both have their uses.

douse, dowse

There seems no good reason why these should be interchangeable as they are in some dictionaries. To **douse** is to saturate with water, as with **dousing** a fire or **dousing** (plunging) something into water or some other liquid. **Dowsing** is what you do with a forked twig or divining rod – locate underground water.

draws, drawers

Draws are small lotteries; **drawers** slide out from cabinets or tables. **Drawers** is also used as a comic alternative to underpants and knickers.

drowned

Check the differences in meaning between these two statements: 'The unfortunate young man drowned in the weir'; 'The unfortunate young man was drowned in the weir.' *The Times* holds that **drowned** means that a person suffocates, usually accidentally, in water or other liquid; but that **was drowned** indicates that another person caused the victim's death by holding the unfortunate's head underwater.

druggist

See **chemist, druggist, pharmacist**

dryer, drier, drily, dryly

By using **dryer** for drying machines (spin dryer, hair dryer) you leave the way clear to use **drier** as the comparative adjective to mean 'more dry'. **Drily** and **dryly** are synonomous.

Due to, owing to

A full account of **because, since, on account of, owing to** and **due to** was given in *Word Check*. Explaining the precise differences between these can turn out to be a wordy business, but Mr Jonathan Cocking, a *Sunday Times* reader from Edgware, Middlesex, cuts through it all: 'A mnemonic I learnt in school always gives the right answer: **Due to** means **caused by**; **Owing to** means **because of**.'

dyke, dike

In the context of female homosexuality, **dyke** (or **dike**), formerly an insulting term for a lesbian, is now being reclaimed and although half-way respectable, use with caution.

dysfunction, malfunction

In the meaning of failure to operate properly, due to some disturbance or deterioration of a part or organ, both mean the same.
Dysfunction is perhaps used more to express organic abnormality.

each other, one another

Many people try to preserve a difference between these: using **each other** for two things; **one another** for more than two. Their usage has, however, become so muddled and intertwined that it's a battle hardly worth fighting.

earthly, earthy

The use of **earthly,** meaning 'real, of the world, material' is virtually confined to clichés like **no earthly chance** and **an earthly paradise.** **Earthy** means characteristic of earth: 'This has an earthy taste'; 'Bill's language is pretty earthy.'

eclectic

See **esoteric, eclectic, exotic**

ecology, environment

Ecology is the study of the relationship between the environment and its inhabitants, human and otherwise. The **environment** defines the external habitat and conditions surrounding an individual or group, human or otherwise.

economic, economical, encomium

Economic relates to economics, the principles governing the production and consumption of goods and services and commercial activity: 'The Government's recent economic policy was founded on optimistic expectations.' To be **economical** is to be thrifty and not wasteful. An **encomium** is a formal eulogy.

educationalist, educationist, educator

There is considerable debate about these but surely **educator** is the simplest and least pompous.

effrontery

See **affront, effrontery**

egregious

See **gregarious, egregious**

elder, older, eldest, oldest

The use of these words is governed by tradition. **Elder** and **eldest** are used primarily for human family relationships; you do not say, 'Toby is the eldest horse in the stables', but you might say, 'Mr French is the firm's elder partner.' **Older** is the comparative of **old**: 'John is the older of the two brothers; I thought Emily was the oldest member of the family but it turns out that Rebecca is the eldest.'

elemental, elementary

Elemental relates to the primal forces of nature: 'The elemental surge of the tides.' **Elementary** means rudimentary, fundamental, basic and simple: 'Elementary, my dear Watson.'

elucidate, explain

Elucidate is merely a fancy word for **explain**.

elude

See **allude, elude**

emend

See **amend, emend**

empirical, imperial

The confusion between these two no doubt arises from the similarity of **emperor** and **empire** to **empirical**, but there is no connection. **Empirical** means making judgements from observation and experience rather than theory. The word that relates to **empire** is **imperial**.

enjoin, join

To **join**, meaning to 'bring together', offers no problems. To **enjoin** is to order, urge or require someone to do something: 'The speaker enjoined the angry gathering to proceed quietly to their homes.'

enormity

Collins' third definition of **enormity** is its informal meaning, 'vastness of size or extent', which is to be avoided. **Enormity** is the quality of extreme wickedness, something monstrous: 'Even the hardened policemen were shocked by the enormity of the crime.'

enrol, enroll

The 1992 brochure of Kingsbridge Community College in Devon invites students to 'enrole' in a variety of courses – including A-Level English. There is no such word. The word the college wanted was **enrol**, which is preferred to **enroll** which is generally used in the US.

envisage, envision

These are near synonyms, but **envision** tends to imply the conception of a possibility rather than an image: 'The minister envisioned a day when everyone, regardless of circumstance, would be adequately housed.' To **envisage** is to form a mental image of something in the future: 'She envisaged her ideal house: a modernised but solid thatched cottage with an old-fashioned garden and orchard.'

epigram, epigraph, epitaph

Dennis Potter's 'The trouble with words is that you never know whose mouths they've been in' is an **epigram**: a pithy, witty slice of wisdom. An **epitaph**, inscribed on a gravestone, sums up the person's life, as in this example commemorating the seventeenth century architect Sir John Vanbrugh:

> Under this stone, reader, survey
> Dear Sir John Vanbrugh's house of clay.
> Lie heavy on him, earth! for he
> Laid many heavy loads on thee.

An **epigraph** is usually a thematic quotation appearing at the beginning of a book, but it can also be an inscription on a statue or building.

epithet

Careful users will observe this word's original meaning: an adjective or phrase expressing some attribute or quality characteristic of a person or thing. Magic Johnson, Chubby Checker, Gorgeous Gussie Moran, Richard the Lionheart and Fatty Arbuckle are all epithets – none of them necessarily disparaging. Today, many, if not most, people regard an **epithet** as abusive: 'She had "stupid bitch" and other epithets hurled at her by the passing lorry drivers.'

equable, equitable

Equable means unvarying and free from extremes: 'As the executive who fields all the complaints, John has the ideal equable temperament.' **Equitable** means fair, impartial and just: 'The insurance company eventually arrived at an equitable settlement.'

erupt, irrupt

To **erupt** is to burst out violently; to **irrupt** is to enter forcibly and violently. The same meanings apply to the nouns, **eruption** and **irruption**.

Eponymous and eponyms

A beguiling word like **eponymous** is bound to attract over-use and, inevitably, misuse. An **eponym** is a name – of a product, place or some creation – that derives from the name of a real or mythical person: **cardigan** (after the 7th Earl of Cardigan); **mesmerise** (after physician F. A. Mesmer); **spoonerism** (after the Rev. W. A. Spooner) and **nosey parker** (after Dr Parker, sixteenth century Archbishop of Canterbury) are just a few of thousands. Simple enough, but difficulties arise with the use of **eponymous**. In a recent Sunday colour magazine a writer made reference to 'the eponymous Mother Seraphima' of the Church of St Seraphim, which is wrongly to credit Mother Seraphima with saintdom. You might, however, see 'the remains of St Seraphim and the eponymous church', which *is* correct usage. Also, it seems, the meaning of **eponymous** has been widened to relate a product to the company that makes it: 'There are, so the WordPerfect Corporation claims, more than 10 million users of its eponymous product.'

esoteric, eclectic, exotic

This trio presents many of us with problems. Something **esoteric** is confined or restricted to a minority who understand it, like Rastafarian slang, the peculiar attractions of trainspotting or, these days, Latin. Something **exotic** is strange, unusual and foreign but it can also mean outrageous and thrilling. An **eclectic** person has the talent and taste to select the best of everything. For the record, the opposite of **esoteric** is **exoteric**, meaning open, popular, everybody's.

euphemism, euphuism

Euphuism looks like **euphemism** spelt wrongly, but it is a word that defines a high-flown, ornate and affected style of writing. A **euphemism** is an inofffensive word or phrase substituted for one considered to be hurtful, unpleasant or embarrassing. **Bathroom** for lavatory, **perspiration** for sweat, **gay** for homosexual, **let go** for sacked, **passed away** for died, **that time** for menstruation, **passing wind** for fart are all common euphemisms. Much so-called politically correct and nondiscriminatory language is also euphemistic.

European Union, European Community, Common Market

Use the former and the abbreviation **EU** rather than **Common Market**, **EEC** or **EC**.

evince, evoke

Both are used in relation to abstractions, such as emotions and visions. To **evince** is to reveal; to **evoke** is to 'summon up': 'She evinced no surprise when confronted by the evidence': 'In his speech he evoked the dream of freedom, independence and nationhood.'

exacerbate, exasperate, aggravate

All three mean 'to make worse' but are used in slightly different ways. **Exacerbate** is customarily applied to things and conditions: 'The almost-forgotten feud between the brothers was now exacerbated by family interference.' **Exasperate** is used to express worsening situations between individuals: 'He finally exasperated me to the point of screaming!' **Aggravate** – which a large number of people believe to mean 'annoy' – is a synonym for **exacerbate** but may sometimes involve a degree of intent and persistence: 'Elizabeth's constant sniping at Jack was carefully calculated to aggravate the situation.'

excoriate, execrate

One old meaning of **excoriate** was 'to flay or to strip the skin' from someone. Today's usage is less physical but no less severe: to denounce or condemn scathingly. To **execrate** is to loathe and detest.

exercise

See **exorcise, exercise**

exhaust, deplete, reduce

Exhaust means to drain, empty, remove and to deplete totally. **Reduce**, in a similar context, means to make smaller in size, number or extent. The odd man out is **deplete**, which, rather unhelpfully, can mean to use up or empty partially or completely. If you intend to write, 'The Anglian reservoirs were depleted before the end of summer', you are inviting confusion. Use **exhausted** or **reduced** to be specific.

exigency, exiguous

Two classic confusables, which is perhaps why you don't see (or even need to use) them too often. An **exigency** is a state of great urgency that requires immediate attention. **Exiguous** means meagre, small: 'The problem with the Somalis, apart from all the natural and man-made disasters, was simply their traditionally exiguous incomes.'

exorcise, exercise

Although there cannot be many unfamiliar with **exercise**, these two are sometimes muddled. Stephen Murray-Smith cites a New South Wales Government leaflet advising car buyers to demand the car's history from the vendor, 'Otherwise, a finance company could exorcise its rights'. To **exorcise** is to attempt to dispel evil spirits from a person or place.

expatiate, expiate

Nasty ones, these. To **expatiate** is to elaborate or enlarge upon a topic in speaking or writing: 'The doctor expatiated on the dangers of bad dietary habits.' To **expiate** is to make amends for some wrong.

expatriate, compatriot

An **expatriate** is a resident in a foreign country; **to expatriate** is to expel a person from a country. A **compatriot** is a fellow countryman: 'He found several compatriots among the British expatriates in Barcelona.'

explain

See **elucidate, explain**

explicit, implicit

To be **explicit** is to be absolutely clear and specific, but something **implicit** is not directly

Extract the extract and other lookalikes

There is a family of words that frequently cause people to pause: words which are spelt the same but are pronounced or accented differently where there is one pronunciation for the noun and another for the verb. An example is **extract**. The **extract** of cod liver oil you may have known in your childhood is pronounced **EX-trakt**, while the process of **extracting** it from the poor cod is pronounced **ex-TRAKT**.

Here are some other fairly common words where the nouns and adverbs look alike but are pronounced differently:

abstract, accent, attribute, collect, combat, compound, compress, conduct, conflict, consort, contest, contract, contrast, convert, convict, defect, desert, detail, digest, discharge, discount, entrance, escort, essay, exploit, export, ferment, import, impress, imprint, incense, increase, insult, object, pervert, present, progress, project, rebel, refuse, second, suspect, survey, transport, transfer.

The following are some adjective-verb lookalikes:

absent, alternate, converse, frequent, intimate, perfect, present.

And, finally, a few noun-adjective lookalikes:

august, compact, content, invalid.

expressed but implied or hinted at. Nevertheless, whatever is **implied** is usually well or instinctively understood: 'The volunteers were only too keenly aware of the implicit dangers in the task ahead.'

extempore

See **impromptu, extempore**

extraneous, extrinsic

Extraneous means 'external or coming from without' but more properly – irrelevant, unrelated or not essential: 'At the enquiry the business about the missing car was considered to be an extraneous issue.' **Extrinsic** has a subtly similar meaning but is applied in the sense of not being an inherent or essential part of something: 'The auctioneer played up the extrinsic contribution of the necklace's previous royal owners to its fame and value.' Its opposite, **intrinsic**, meaning an essential part of something, is more common.

facts, true facts, factitious

Facts are verified or observable truths, events that have actually happened, or things that have existed or are real. To say **true facts** is tautological. Something **factitious**, on the other hand, is false or artificial: 'The candidate won solely by the factitious nature of his campaign.'

fair, fayre

Does the ubiquity of **fayre** to denote a country or charity fair or fête indicate a desire to revert to fifteenth-century English? More likely it is a

symptom of the Ye Olde Syndrome, the quest
for the quaint – to be discouraged.

fatal, fated, fateful

Fatal primarily means causing or resulting in
death; **fated** means doomed. **Fateful** is the
most pregnant of the group, suggesting all kinds
of ominous portents beyond anyone's control
including death, disaster and ruin: 'From that
fateful encounter sprang a history of hate that
engulfed the two neighbouring states.'

faze

See **phase, faze**

feel, think

'I feel I should leave now', or usages similar to
this example are common enough. But . . . **feel**?
In most cases the user means **think** or **believe**:
'I think/believe I should leave now.' But if a
person is at a party and realises that he or she is
under the weather, **feel** would no doubt be
appropriate. **Feel** is over-used as a synonym for
think, which it isn't. Just **think** about it, that's
all.

fervent, fervid, fervour

Fervour is an intense feeling, a passion, from
which springs **fervent**, meaning to be keenly
enthusiastic, ardent and passionate. **Fervid** is
synonymous in most dictionaries but it tends to
be used to suggest a heightened, more
passionate, even incandescent fervour for which
the little used **perfervid** is really the correct
word.

fictional, fictitious

Something **fictional** relates to a fiction, a work of the imagination – a novel, play or movie: 'He referred to the fictional account of his grandfather's life in "The Moon and Sixpence".' Something **fictitious** is untrue or not genuine: 'I'm tired of hearing her obviously fictitious excuses for being late each morning.'

find out

See **ascertain, find out**

finial, filial

A **finial** is an ornament at the top of a spire, gable or piece of furniture. **Filial** relates to a son or daughter: 'He expected, and received, daily displays of filial devotion.'

first, firstly

It's not worth getting into a tizz over **firstly** as many grammarians have in objecting to **firstly, secondly, thirdly**, etc. Use it if you wish, or even **first, secondly, thirdly** and so on. But shorter and neater (and avoiding ninety-ninethly) is the formula: **first, second, third** . . .

flat, condominium, apartment

While usage is sometimes flexible, a **flat** in the UK and other places, like Australia, is an **apartment** in the US, although the latter is becoming synonymous for a swanky flat and can be a 'duplex' (on two floors) or a 'triplex' (on three). A **condominium**, more common in the US than elsewhere, is a building of flats where the owners share the cost and responsibilities for the upkeep of the whole building and its facilities.

flautist, flutist

In Britain a flute player is a **flautist**; **flutist** is the US term.

flora and fauna

Unlike similar Latin nouns these aren't plural; they're collective nouns. The plurals are floras and faunas.

flotsam, jetsam, ligan

These all come from a ship, items that either float off (**flotsam**), are jettisoned or thrown off (**jetsam**) or sink to the bottom (**lagan** or **ligan**). The question is, how do you tell when you find them?

flounder

See **founder, flounder**

fluorescent, florescence

A **fluorescent** substance absorbs radiation of a particular wavelength and converts it to light, called **fluorescence**. **Florescence** is the process of flowering in a plant.

fob, foist

There is not much between these two except that usage seems to favour **foist** as meaning to deceptively pass off something fake or inferior as genuine and valuable, or to impose an unwanted item or task onto someone: 'That supervisor deliberately foisted this lousy job on me.' **Fob** means to put off by evasion, and is usually accompanied by **off**: 'She won't fob me off with that weak excuse again.'

forceful, forcible, forced

Forcible and **forced** are near adjectival synonyms, the latter more common, but both indicate the use of force: 'The evidence indicated a forced entry.' **Forceful** means powerful and persuasive: 'His advocacy at the trial was both thoughtful and forceful.'

forego, forgo

To **forego** means to precede; to **forgo** means to abstain or do without.

former, latter

Many people still stick to a usage rule that these should only be used when referring to two people or things: 'The doctor recommended brandy and lemon with lots of the former'; but 'The doctor recommended brandy, lemon and aspirin – with lots of brandy.'

forward, forwards

Forward is preferred, with the exception of one or two usages like 'backwards and forwards'.

founder, flounder

Flounder means to struggle helplessly: 'After a series of interruptions the speaker floundered for several minutes.' If you **founder**, however, you've really had it; it means to sink.

frantic, frenetic

Someone **frantic** is to some degree frenzied, over-excited, hysterical and agitated. **Frenetic** is a close synonym but its roots from both Greek and Latin link it more to the mind and insanity; perhaps best reserved for indicating a wild, deranged frenzy.

fruition, completion

Fruition implies the enjoyment of fulfilment and success. **Completion** is the state of being complete: 'The completion of the project signalled the fruition of his life's work.'

Unfamiliar facts about fulsome

'Listening to the fulsome praise heaped upon her by the president, the champion glowed with pride.' Someone should have tipped off the poor girl; today's meaning of **fulsome** is – embarrassingly, even disgustingly excessive, insincere, distasteful, nauseating.

Fulsome is often misused to mean lavish but perhaps, reviewing its etymology over the past 800 years, it's no surprise. In the thirteenth century it did mean full and copious but by the fourteenth had come to imply fat and overgrown. By the fifteenth the word was even less attractive (gross, satiated) and in 1604 the *Oxford English Dictionary* records that it meant 'morally foul and obscene'. The present usage has remained fairly constant since towards the end of the seventeenth century.

---

funds

See **money, monies, funds, cash**

fustian, fusty

Fustian is used mostly in the literary sense of being pretentious, pompous and bombastic. **Fusty** means smelling damp and mouldy and, figuratively, being stale and old-fashioned.

futility, fatuity, futurity

Futility means total lack of purpose, point and success. **Fatuity** is complacency, inanity, smug stupidity. **Futurity** is the odd one out and is a fancy word for 'the future'.

gaff, gaffe

A **gaff** is a fishing pole with a hook on it; a **gaffe** is a social blunder or an indiscreet remark.

Gallic, Gaelic

Gallic (from Gaul, formerly France) relates to France and its people. **Gaelic** refers to Celtic descendents (Scots, Irish, Isle of Man) and their languages.

gelatin, gelatine

Generally, the British use **gelatine**, and the Americans **gelatin**.

gender

See **sex and gender**

generous

See **prodigal, generous**

genial, congenial, congenital

To be **genial** is to be friendly, pleasant and good-tempered; to be **congenial** is to relate to and share your friendliness with others of similar disposition: 'The atmosphere during the trip was wonderfully congenial.' **Congenital** relates to any non-heredity abnormality acquired before or during birth.

get, acquire, obtain, secure

Get is such a powerful, versatile but simple word
that we often fall over ourselves trying to find a
smarter substitute. Usually there isn't one.
Gower hates **acquire**, but you can use it in a
sort of shifty sense: 'He acquired it from the back
of a lorry.' There's not much call for **obtain**.
Secure is like **get** plus a **favour**: 'I've secured
you two tickets for the match tomorrow.'

geyser, geezer

A **geyser** is an active hot spring and used to be
(in the UK) a domestic gas water-heater. A
geezer is any old man, but **the geezer** is 'the
boss'.

gibe

See **jibe, gibe, gybe**

gilt, guilt

Gilt is the result of gilding: covering with gold
or something that looks like it. **Guilt** is the
product of moral or criminal wrong-doing.

give

See **donate, give**

got, gotten, has got

Gotten travelled with the settlers from Britain
to America where it is now standard usage.
Here, although we've retained **forget/forgotten**
and the biblical **beget/begotten**, the furrowed
brow brigade has effectively kept **gotten** out of
modern Britain. Here **got** is the past participle
of **to get** as well as being the form used for the
past tense, and perhaps we use it too much:
'She's got a great voice'; 'They've got a nerve!'

Used informally in speech there's little to complain about, but when spelled out many people find it grating: 'She has got a great voice'; 'They have got a nerve!' With **has got** and **have got** the objection disappears when you drop **got**: 'She has a great voice'; 'I have to go' instead of 'I have got to go'. There are no firm rules for **got**, but sentences often seem more elegant without it.

gradation, graduation

A **gradation** is a gradual progression of stages: in size, tone, sound or degree, often imperceptible. In this context, a **graduation** is a progression of measuring marks or divisions.

gratuitous, gratuity

Sometimes confused with **gratitude**, **gratuitous** indicates something given free and unrequested. Its usual use today is to define something that's unnecessary and uncalled-for: 'The pair traded gratuitous insults for half an hour.' A **gratuity** is a gift, usually money, for services rendered.

green paper

See **white paper, green paper**

gregarious, egregious

These were once opposites: **gregarious**, meaning enjoying the company of others and tending to flock together; and **egregious**, meaning separate from the flock, or outstanding. But while **gregarious** has retained its original meaning, **egregious** is now used almost exclusively in a derogatory sense to mean blatant, obtrusive, notorious, bald-faced: 'I've

never met such an egregious liar in all my life.'
Pronounced **ih-GREE-jus**.

grisly, grizzly
Grisly means gruesome; something **grizzly**, usually applied to hair, is grey or streaked with grey.

guilt
See **gilt, guilt**

gybe
See **jibe, gibe, gybe**

habit, habitual
A **habit** is an established or usual custom, so the term 'usual habit' is a redundancy and a cliché; so is 'customary habit'. **Habitual** is the adjective, meaning by habit: 'He was an habitual drinker.'

hale, hail
These two words come in four guises: **hale** the adjective, meaning robust and healthy; **hale** the verb, meaning to haul or drag; **hail** the noun, meaning frozen rain; and **hail** the verb, meaning to greet enthusiastically. Know those and you'll know how to use them in such expressions as: 'He was haled into court'; 'He was all hail-fellow-well-met'; 'At eighty-five he was still hale and hearty.'

hanged, hung
A person is **hanged** (by the neck until dead); a picture is **hung**.

hanger, hangar

A **hanger** is the wire contraption on which you hang clothes; a **hangar** is for housing aircraft.

happen

See **transpire, happen, occur**

harangue, tirade

A **harangue** is a loud, forceful, long and eventually tedious speech: 'He harangued the crowd for two interminable hours.' A **tirade** is much the same but angrier and vituperative.

harbinger

See **bell-wether, harbinger**

harmful

See **deleterious, harmful**

Hebrew

See **Jewish, Hebrew, Yiddish**

helpmate, helpmeet

A **helpmate** is a helpful friend, companion, husband or wife. A **helpmeet** is exactly the same and derives from the biblical 'I will make him an helpe meet for him.' (**Genesis ii:18**)

histology, history

History we all know; **histology** is the study of plant and animal tissues.

historic, historical

Something significant that has a place in history is **historic**: 'The long-delayed meeting will be one of the great historic events of our time.'

Historical relates to events of the past: 'The novel was based on historical evidence.'

hoi polloi

Many believe this Greek expression refers to the rich elite; what it means really is 'the common people' and is usually applied in a derogatory sense **by** the rich elite: 'Who knows or cares what *hoi polloi* are doing.'

holistic, holy

Holistic has nothing to do with God or any sacred deity, and thus has no connection with **holy**. **Holistic** refers to the doctrine that the whole of a system is greater than the sum of its parts. In treating human disorders, holistic medicine, for example, considers the whole person and not just individual organs.

holocaust, Holocaust

A **holocaust** is an act of terrible destruction, but since, with its capital letter, it has come to mean and symbolise the Nazi genocide of the Jews in World War II, use with caution for fear of being misunderstood.

home, house

A **house**, as the saying goes, is not a **home**, and therefore to many people it seems reasonable to say that you can build, buy or sell a **house**, but you can't buy or sell a **home**.

hoodoo

See **voodoo, hoodoo**

Horrible, horrendous, horrifying, horrific . . . and horripilation

How do you separate these? Most people don't bother and use them willy-nilly with the result that they are all, more often than not, used incorrectly: 'It looked horrible!' (my new hair-do); 'It was horrendous' (the English exam)' 'It was absolutely horrific' (the bare-knuckle ride).

But now everyone has a new and virginal word to corrupt: **horripilation**: '. . . one feels throughout a distinct horripilation, a quavering anticipation of something about to spring on us over the next page.' (*Sunday Times* book review) **Horripilation** is the bristling of short bodily hairs; in other words, goose-flesh.

host, hosted

Hosted is not much recognised as a word and when it is the dictionary labels it as informal. But as a substitute verb for **present**, as in television – 'He was hired to host the new game-show'; 'She hosted the quiz with great skill' – it has acquired something more than jargon status.

hullo, hello

Originally it was **hallo** or **halloo**, now generally **hello** is used; **hullo** is an alternative.

human, humanity, humane, inhuman, inhumane

Human and **humanity** relate to the human race, mankind, and the words are generally used with favourable intent. To be **humane** is one of the civilising qualities of mankind and means to be kind and merciful. Conversely, an **inhuman** person lacks the qualities of humankind; to be **inhumane** is to be unfeeling, cruel and brutal.

humanist, humanitarian

A **humanist** believes in the superiority of human ideals – literature, philosphy, history, culture – over religious beliefs. A **humanitarian** is a kind, philanthropic person with the interests of mankind at heart.

humus, hummus, houmous, hoummos

Humus is decayed organic matter in soil; **hummus, houmous** or **hoummos** is a chick pea puree which originated in the Middle East.

It is I, it is me; you and I, you and me

It is I, or **It is me**? **Between you and I**, or **Between you and me**? With the first pair, just about everyone accepts that the **It is I** construction sounds affected and although **It is me** is regarded as colloquial it also sounds right. But this doesn't mean that you can write 'Doreen and me sat next to each other'; here it is simpler to reconstruct: 'Doreen sat next to me.' In the past many people dealt with the problem pair **between you and I/between you and me** by quoting from the *Merchant of Venice*: 'All debts are cleared between you and I', claiming that although they vaguely remembered that 'I'

shouldn't follow a preposition, if it was good
enough for Will it was good enough for them.
A simple rule is to omit mentally the 'you and'
bit from such constructions as 'between you
and I/me' and 'after you and I/me' when you
quickly see that 'between I' and 'after I' is
plainly wrong.

identical to, identical with

Identical with is the originally correct usage,
although today little fuss is made about
identical to.

ilk, of that ilk

The traditional Scottish meaning of **of that ilk** is
'of the same name' and it has an extremely
narrow application, as in 'Gordon of that ilk',
signifying that Gordon is laird of the estate of
the same name. Now **ilk** is commonly used to
mean 'of the same sort or class'.

ill

See **sick, sickly, ill**

imbue

See **inculcate, imbue**

impassable, impassible

Something **impassable** means it cannot be
passed or travelled over: 'During winter the old
mountain track is quite impassable.' **Impassible**
is not a variant spelling but a different word
meaning insensible to injury and pain.

impel

See **compel, impel**

imperial
See **empirical, imperial**

implicit
See **explicit, implicit**

impromptu, extempore
Both mean spontaneous and unpremeditated but **extempore** is customarily reserved to describe an off-the-cuff speech.

improve, ameliorate
Ameliorate is frequently wrongly used to mean remove, mitigate, alleviate, lessen, nullify or neutralise. It means to improve or to make better. Avoid ambiguity by using **improve**.

incapable, unable
There is a difference between the two for those who wish to preserve it. **Incapable** means lacking in ability, capacity or power to accomplish something; 'incompetent' would be a near synonym: 'Fred was utterly incapable of singing in tune.' But with a statement like, 'Fred was unable to climb the stairs' we are left in some doubt; Fred probably could climb the stairs when he sobers up. **Unable** implies an inability to do something at a particular time or in some special circumstance.

inchoate
See **chaotic, inchoate**

inculcate, imbue
'His father had inculcated him in most of the rules of hunting'; 'She was thoroughly inculcated with Theodora's legendary wisdom.'

Both these usages are common but wrong. You cannot **inculcate** people, only ideas: 'Mr Simon inculcated a new sense of purpose in the entire staff.' But you may **imbue** or inspire a person with ideas: 'His father had imbued him with a sense of pride'; 'She was thoroughly imbued with Theodora's legendary wisdom.'

in-depth

As in 'an **in-depth** analysis', a cliché to avoid.

inequity, iniquity

Inequity is injustice; an **inequitable** situation is unjust and unfair. An **iniquity** is also an injustice, but one that is grievous and wicked.

inestimable

See **invaluable, inestimable**

infect, infest

To **infect** is to cause an infection or to contaminate; to **infest** is to overrun in dangerous numbers: 'The infestation of lice was undoubtedly the cause of the infection.'

informant, informer

An **informant** supplies information; an **informer** provides information with the intention of incriminating someone.

infringe, infringe on, infringe upon

'The man infringed the law and paid the price' is correct; **infringe** means to break or violate and thus either **on** or **upon** is redundant. But many of us feel the need for the prepositions when **infringe** is used to mean 'to trespass or encroach upon': 'The farmer's animals

constantly infringed upon the municipal park.'
Keep your nerve and leave them out.

in heat, on heat, in season
All are acceptable (especially to the animals concerned).

in lieu of, instead of
If you accept the principle of using foreign words and expressions only in the absence of a suitable English equivalent, use **instead of**.

insofar as, in so far as
'In so far as the inflation rate is concerned, prices will inevitably respond' is still general English usage, although the American **insofar** seems to be rapidly gaining ground.

instinct, intuition
Instinct is a natural impulse triggered by some stimulus; **intuition** is an unconscious, non-reasoning mental awareness. 'Sensing a movement, he instinctively stepped back'; 'She intuitively realised she would never feel comfortable with David.'

intense, intensive
The two are different. **Intense** should be used to describe extremes: **intense** heat, **intense** power, **intense** aroma. **Intensive** is about concentration: concentrated medical effort (**intensive** care); a concentrated murder investigation (**intensive** enquiries).

internecine
From its original meaning of bloody carnage and slaughter **internecine** is primarily used now to describe a conflict that is mutually destructive.

internment, interment

Internment is detaining and confining someone, usually for security reasons during a conflict or a war. An **interment** is a burial.

intrigue, intriguing

Although there is still some resistance to the wider use of **intrigue** meaning to arouse curiosity and interest, this has now substantially overtaken the original meaning of 'to plot secretly'. The same applies to **intriguing**.

intrinsic

See **extraneous**, **extrinsic**

invaluable, inestimable

Invaluable means priceless – something so valuable its worth is difficult or impossible to estimate. **Inestimable**, meaning 'beyond estimation', is a synonym but tends to be used to describe abstract rather than material qualities: 'The speaker praised her for her inestimable contribution to the project.'

inveigh, inveigle

To **inveigh** is to denounce or to speak bitterly about something: 'The Opposition leader inveighed against the injustice of the Poll Tax.' Note that **inveigh** is followed by **against**. To **inveigle** is to convince or persuade by trickery.

invoke, evoke

Two well-worn confusables! To **invoke** is to appeal to or call upon someone – often God – for help or inspiration: 'He fell to his knees and invoked the wrath of Allah upon his enemies.' To **evoke** is to summon or recall some feeling or

memory: 'The plaintive dirge evoked in her a
rush of memories of her Highland childhood.'
See also **evince, evoke**.

ion, iron

The confusion probably arises in the UK because
these are pronounced similarly. An **ion** is an
electrically charged atom or group of atoms; **iron**
is, of course, the metal.

iterate

See **reiterate, iterate**

-ize, -ise

Only a handful of words require the **-ize** spelling
(size, prize, capsize) while many have always
taken **-ise** (advise, arise, despise, devise,
exercise, raise, rise, surprise are just a few). This
has led to a tendency to favour **-ise** in British
English although **-ize** is standard in the US.
The Sunday Times and *The Times* subscribe to
-ise endings but there are many publishers who
for etymological reasons retain **-ize**.

jejune

Here is a word with a meaning in motion. Two
decades ago dictionaries gave its primary
definition as 'lacking in substance; insipid, dry,
meagre'. If someone said 'Catherine's laborious
essay is jejune in the extreme', you were being
told the essay was empty, dull and without
interest. But that's not what the word signifies to
most people today. That same sentence now
would most likely be trying to suggest that the
essay was naïve and immature. If you wish to
avoid being misunderstood, avoid **jejune**.

jetsam
See **flotsam, jetsam, ligan**

jersey
See **sweater, jersey, jumper, pullover, etc**.

Jewish, Hebrew, Yiddish
While there remains a sensitivity about **Jew** being a pejorative term, it is preferable to euphemisms like 'a Jewish person' and is generally preferred by the Jewish community anyway: 'My fellow Jews approve it,' wrote one reader of the first edition of *Word Check*. **Jewess** is discouraged, however; Jewish woman is preferred. **Hebrew** and **Yiddish** are languages spoken by Jews; **Hebrew** is the official language of Israel, while **Yiddish** is a Hebrew-influenced vernacular version of German.

jibe, gibe, gybe
To **gibe** means to taunt or jeer, and that is the favoured spelling; **jibe** is an alternative. **Gybe** is a yachting term with, again, **jibe** as an alternative spelling.

join
See **enjoin, join**

judgment, judgement
Many newspapers in Britain now drop the 'e'.

jumper
See **sweater, jersey, jumper, pullover, etc**.

The joys of jargon, slang, colloquialism, vernacular, argot, cant, lingua franca and gobbledegook

Jargon is a collective word for mini-languages understood by a small number of people. Pick up a computer magazine and you will find yourself face to face with **jargon**. **Jargon** is often occupational:

SCIENCE	chaology, cyborg, entropy, double helix, quark
COMPUTING	wysiwyg, bus, dump, download, interface, pixel
FINANCE	call, bull, junk bond, OTC, white knight, spread
MEDICAL	bronk, DNR, perrla, scoop, MFC

Slang is a separate vocabulary from the standard language, often used by specific social types (Cockney) or during a period (wartime). Sometimes called 'unconventional English', some **slang** words disappear, some keep their status, while many make it to dictionary respectability.

junction, juncture

A **junction** is a place where several things meet: roads, railway lines, electrical cables, etc. A **juncture** is a moment in time like a pause, a crisis or a turning point: 'At this juncture it is essential that we review the situation.'

jury, juror, jurist

A **jury** is composed of members of the jury, or **jurors**. A **jurist** is a general term to describe

A **colloquialism** is an unconventional word or phrase you'd use casually in conversation; **vernacular** is the native spoken language or dialect of a particular group or race. **Argot**, formerly the 'language of thieves', is now a synonym for **jargon**; **cant** means any hypocritically pious language. **Lingua franca** defines a language used by people of different mother tongues to communicate among themselves; pidgin, for example, is the **lingua franca** of the people of Papua New Guinea who are divided by hundreds of separate languages.

Gobbledegook is pretentious, pompous, utterly confusing and obscure language, instantly recognisable when you fail to understand it: 'If you only pay a charge as a result of a charge you paid in a previous charging period . . .'

anyone well versed in law but including legal graduates, students and writers.

ketchup, sauce, chutney, pickle

Ketchup is a vinegar-based condiment, usually tomato flavoured, and often distributed directly on to food from a bottle; **catsup** is a little-used alternative spelling. With our modern preoccupation with cooking and restaurant eating, a **sauce** is increasingly a piquant liquid accompaniment to a cooked dish. **Chutney** consists of coarsely cut fruit and vegetables preserved by cooking with vinegar, sugar, salt and spices. **Pickle** consists of vegetables – onions, cauliflower, etc. – preserved in vinegar or brine.

kind of, sort of

The trick with **kind of** is to recognise when you need the plural form: 'This kind of book gives publishing a bad name'; 'These are the kinds of books that give publishing a bad name.' The same applies to **sort of** and **sorts of**.

The last joyride

Can a word be deliberately abandoned ... sent to Coventry? Take the case of **joyride**. A typical dictionary definition is: 'A ride taken for pleasure in a car, especially in a stolen car driven recklessly.' (*Collins Softback*, 1992) Unfortunately for many people, especially the victims of so-called **joyriders**, the result of such rides is far from joyous. The toll of murder-by-joyride in the UK has mounted to such an extent that the *Daily Mirror* decided in 1993 to ban the word: 'This is the last time the word "joyride" will appear in the *Daily Mirror*.' For a word that now means almost the opposite of what it originally meant, it is perhaps not a bad idea. But what might take its place? How about **car thief** or **car killer**?

kinky, quirky

Within a couple of decades, **kinky**, originally meaning eccentric or bizarre, has come to mean unusual or abnormal sexual behaviour. **Quirky** is safer if you wish to describe someone or something as peculiar, unconventional and unpredictable.

knell, knoll

A **knell** is the tolling of a bell that announces a death or a funeral; a **knoll** is a small, usually round, hill.

labour

See **belabour, labour**

landslide, landslip

Both are synonymous when referring to a mass of earth or rock giving way, but only **landslide** is used to dramatise an overwhelming election victory.

laspe, elapse

Lapse can mean a slight slip or failure – 'We all suffer from the occasional lapse of memory' – a gradual falling or decline – 'They watched as she lapsed into unconsciousness' – or to become ineffective or to expire – 'Unfortunately, their insurance policy had lapsed.' **Lapse** can also indicate the passing of time, which is where it can overlap with the usage of **elapse**: 'Time lapses slowly on that particular journey'; 'Elapsed time at the half-way mark of the race was three hours, thirteen minutes.'

last, latest

'Have you read Salman Rushdie's last book?'
Sounds ominous. What the speaker meant was,
'Have you read Salman Rushdie's latest book?'
Use **last** only when you mean to indicate
finality: 'My father travelled on the last horse-drawn tram in London.'

laudable, laudatory

Laudable means deserving praise; **laudatory**
means expressing praise. **Laudable** is often
used to express worthiness rather than
unqualified approval: 'The committee's efforts,
though laudable, were ultimately a waste of time.'

Lend, loan

A reader's letter to *The Times* reads: 'In my post
today I received a letter from a local
headteacher, offering the use of his school's
facilities. Apart from various grammatical and
spelling errors, his letter invited my firm to
"loan" his school's video. I do not know whether
the concept of borrowing and lending is included
in the national curriculum, but if headteachers
are unable to master this simple idea, what hope
is there for their pupils?'

What the headteacher should have known is
that a **loan** is a financial transaction; you raise
a **loan**, but **lend** a video. What he presumably
intended was to invite the reader's firm to **borrow**
his school's video.

lavatory, toilet

These days the once basic **lavatory** is regarded by many as an affectation; **toilet** is more or less standard. Avoid the US euphemism **bathroom** which can lead to inanities like 'Look, Felix is scratching at the door – he wants to go to the bathroom.'

leading question

A **leading question** is phrased in a way that tends to steer or lead the person being asked to give the desired answer. 'Have you ever seen this man before?' is a fair question. 'Is it not a fact that you have known this man for years?' is a **leading question**. **Leading questions** are regarded as unfair in law and are often disallowed.

learned, learnt

Although **learned** expresses the past tense of **learn**, usage prefers **learnt**, leaving the way clear for **learned** (pronounced **LER-nud**) as the adjective meaning 'having great knowledge'.

legend

See **allegory, fable, myth, parable, legend**

lessee, lessor

A **lessee** leases property from the owner, the **lessor**.

liberal, Liberal, libertarian, libertine

If you are **liberal** you are generous, tolerant, open and receptive to ideas and a champion of individual freedom. If you are a **Liberal** or former **Liberal** you are or were a member of (in Britain) the Liberal Party; a **Liberal**

Democrat is a member of the Liberal Democratic Party. A **libertarian** believes in freedom of thought and speech, while – careful here – a **libertine** is a thoroughly immoral and dissolute philanderer.

licentious, licentiate

Licentious means sexually unrestrained; a **licentiate** is someone holding a professional certificate of competence or a licence to practise some professional discipline.

like, as, as if, such as

For many of us, using **like** to introduce a comparison induces vague discomfort: 'My mother can't get through a busy day like she used to'; 'At the outset it looked like our team could win but fate decreed otherwise'; 'I prefer the early German composers, like Bach.' Of these, only the middle example is incorrect (it should be **as if** or **as though**); the first is correct although some would prefer **as**; and so is the last example although, again, many writers would substitute **such as** for **like**. Grammatically, **like** as a conjunction should not be followed by a subject and verb: 'It looks like Irene will win top honours' is wrong; if your grammar is rusty then your ear should tell you.

lira, lire

The Italian currency unit **lira** is singular; **lire** is plural.

litany, liturgy

A **litany** in the Christian religion is a repetitious prayer to which there is a fixed response by the congregation. The **Litany** (caps) is the prayer contained in the *Book of Common Prayer*. If you use **litany** in a non-religious sense to mean a long, repetitious and tedious list or speech, make it clear. A **liturgy** is the prescribed ritual of church worship.

Literally

Although **literally** was discussed in the first *Word Check* book, the flagrant, even wilful, misuse and abuse of this word continues unabated. The main offenders are those who, when using **literally**, mean **not literally** or **figuratively** or **metaphorically**, and each week the satirical magazine *Private Eye* parades a cautionary collection of examples: 'William Byrd, who literally had the ear of Elizabeth the First . . .' (Classic-FM announcer); 'Everyone has their ears glued to their radios – quite literally' (BBC); 'Blackburn Rovers are now taking Brian Clough's team literally to the cleaners' (Piccadilly Gold Radio); 'Here under the roof at Earls Court is quite literally the world of boating' (radio announcer). You have been warned.

---

livid, lurid

'His angry, livid face blazed with the intensity of a furnace.' The imagery is certainly dramatic but **livid** here, used to indicate redness, is the wrong word. **Livid** means discoloured, as with a bruise, and if it indicates a colour at all it is bluish-grey. **Lurid** is also sometimes used to convey something red, glowing or fiery; in fact in colour terms it means yellowish, pale and wan. **Lurid** is best used for its primary meaning which is vivid, shocking, sensational: 'They gasped as they listened to all the lurid details.'

loath, loth, loathe

Both **loath** and **loth** are equally acceptable to mean unwilling or reluctant. **Loathe** is from an entirely different word family and means to feel intense hatred and disgust: 'He loathed the very idea of going into hospital.'

locale, location, locality

A **locale** is a place which has a relationship with some event, a venue: 'He inspected the locale of the robbery, the murder and the getaway.' A **location** is a place where something is sited: 'This is the location of the new factory.' A **locality** is an area or district.

loggia, logia

A **loggia** is a gallery or porch supported by columns; **logia** (plural) are the collected sayings of Christ.

look up

The idiomatic **look up** can mean 'refer to'; 'to improve' ('Things are beginning to look up'); 'to have respect for' ('I've always looked up to him'); and 'to make contact' ('We'll look you up next time we're in town'). Use judiciously to avoid misunderstandings; a sign in the window of a Sydney bookstore urged potential customers of Scottish descent to 'Look up your clan's tartan'.

lubricious, lugubrious

Lubricious means lewd and lecherous; **lugubrious** means dismal and mournful.

lumbar, lumber

The **lumbar** region is at the lower end of the spine; **lumber** is sawn timber.

luxuriant, luxurious, luxuriate

Luxuriant means prolific, lush, rich and abundant: 'Lisa had the most luxuriant hair.' Something **luxurious** is sumptuous and usually costly; to **luxuriate** is to revel in pleasure: 'She spent most of the evening luxuriating in the Jacuzzi.'

macrocosm

See **microcosm, macrocosm**

mad, angry

Although **mad** defenders quote the Bible and Shakespeare, using **mad** to mean **angry**, it plainly doesn't. Not yet, anyway, in British English. It means insane.

mafia, Mafia

The **Mafia** (cap) is the infamous international secret organisation founded in Sicily. The word is now also in use generally to denote a powerful clique or group: 'Despite the mergers the firm is still run by the Glasgow mafia.'

malfunction

See **dysfunction, malfunction**

More on majority

Although points about using **majority** and **minority** were made in the first *Word Check*, many readers have asked whether these nouns take singular or plural verbs. Is it 'The majority of the books in the library are never read', or 'is never read'?

The answer lies in the sense indicated by the sentence. If the majority consists of a group (keeping in mind that **majority** and **minority** apply only to entities that can be counted) or bloc then singular would be appropriate: 'His view was that the government's majority was likely to be substantial.' If, on the other hand the majority emphasises individuals, use plural verbs: 'The majority of Eskimos are meat-eaters.' In the sentence about the library, the subject is about books – many books – so the majority 'are never read' is preferred.

mannequin, mannikin

A **mannequin** displaying clothes can be ravishingly live at a fashion show or an inanimate dummy in a shop window. A **mannikin** is a dwarf or very small man, and also a movable model of the human figure, usually reduced in scale.

manqué, marque

Manqué means unfulfilled, failed, would-be: 'Like many members of the Groucho Club he was just a writer *manqué*.' The word, being French, is customarily italicised. A *marque*, also from the French, is a brand or make, usually of a car.

marginal, minimal, slight

Something **marginal** is close to some lower limit: 'The farmers complained about the marginal profit yielded by the new season's potato crop.' Although many dictionaries now allow a secondary meaning of 'small, insignificant, minimal, slight', thoughtful users will stick to the primary meaning.

marriage with, marriage to

The invitation from Buckingham Palace reads: 'Wedding Breakfast following the Marriage of The Prince of Wales with Lady Diana Spencer.' So there you have it; a marriage is after all a union, which suggests **with** rather than **to**.

marten, martin

The **marten** is a furry, flesh-eating weasel-like animal; the **martin** is one of the swallow family.

mawkish, maudlin

Mawkish means sickeningly sentimental, insipid, soppy – yuk! **Maudlin** means a state of tearful, boozy sentimentality.

maxim, axiom

A **maxim** is a concise saying expressing a recognised truth; an **axiom** is a generally accepted principle used as a basis for reasoning or argument.

mayday, May Day

Mayday, the SOS distress signal, is from the French *m'aidez*, meaning 'help me'. **May Day** is the holiday on May 1 each year.

mean, mien

Mean has many meanings but **mien** has only one: **mien** is a person's bearing, appearance or expression.

meaningful

Although according to the *Oxford English Dictionary* **meaningful** has been around since the 1850s it has been around an awful lot since the 1960s when it became an 'in' word. Cautious writers give it a miss, preferring more specific adjectives such as important, significant, far-reaching, valid, critical, valuable, etc.

meantime, meanwhile

Some writers resist using **meantime** as an adverb – 'Meantime, we'll pursue the first objective' – on the grounds that it is first and foremost a noun – 'In the meantime, we'll pursue the first objective.' Both **meanwhile** and **meantime** are in fact interchangeable and have been since Shakespeare's day: 'Meantime, let wonder seem familiar.'

mecca, Mecca

Mecca, birthplace of Muhammed, is the holiest city of Islam; **mecca** (lower case) is used to describe a centre of aspiration or activity: 'St Andrews is the mecca for all true golfing addicts.'

mediate

See **arbitrate, mediate**

Melodic mischief-makers

Melody is a succession of musical notes forming a recognisable sequence: the **tune. Harmony** is the sounding together of combinations of musical notes as **chords. Rhythm** is the regular repetition of sound and stress: the **beat. Counterpoint** is the weaving together of two or more melodic strands. The **lyric** is the words of the song; the **book** is the text – the spoken words and words of songs – for a musical or an opera.

ménage, manège
A **ménage** consists of the members of a household; **manège** means horsemanship; the art of training horses and riders.

metal, mettle
It may surprise you to know that these are often confused. **Metal** is the mineral product (gold, copper, iron, etc.); **mettle** means spirit or courage: 'They all knew the contest would test his mettle.'

microcosm, macrocosm
A **macrocosm** is a whole, an entire unified structure, such as the universe. A **microcosm** is a system on a small scale, a structure in miniature: 'In Gilbert White's mind, Selborne was a microcosm of the world as it then existed.'

mistrust
See **distrust, mistrust**

moat, mote

A **moat** is a ditch filled with water to protect a fortification such as a castle; a **mote** is a tiny speck: 'The sun made bright yellow shafts through the dust motes.'

mollify

See **nullify, mollify**

moment in time, point in time

'At this moment/point in time . . .' is a cliché and also a redundancy or pleonasm. Use **moment**.

momentary, momentarily, momentous

Momentary is the adjective and means lasting only a moment; **momentarily** is the adverb meaning just for a moment, for an instant: 'She was prone to suffer from momentary lapses of memory'; 'As I went to meet him I was momentarily confused.' **Momentous** means of great significance or consequence.

money, monies, funds, cash

Money is a singular noun and it remains singular no matter how much money is involved: a million pounds is still **money**. **Moneys** is the rare plural but **monies**, though archaic, is more common: 'Nearly half of the monies set aside for the projects has been spent.' **Cash** is ready money; **funds** are available resources including, of course, **money**.

moot, moot point

Although **moot** is usually encountered in the phrase **moot point**, meaning a point worth arguing about, **moot** is perfectly capable of acting for itself: 'The students agreed unanimously that the issue of alleged immorality at the University was moot' – in other words the issue was ripe for debate.

moribund

Moribund is commonly misused to convey a state of dormancy, inactivity or sluggishness. Its true meaning is far more dramatic: something **moribund** is at the point of death or extinction.

mortgagee, mortgagor

A **mortgagee** provides the loan; **a mortgagor** borrows the money.

Muslim, Moslem, Islam, Islamic

Muslim is now preferred to **Moslem**; **Muslims** are followers of **Islam**, the religion. **Islamic** is the appropriate adjective when referring to such things as Islamic writing, Islamic art, etc.

myth

See **allegory, fable, myth, parable, legend**

naught

See **nought, naught**

nautical, naval

Nautical refers to anything to do with ships, shipping, seamen and navigation; **naval** relates to a country's navy, its ships, personnel and activities.

nemesis

Frequently misused to mean fate or destiny or even some adversary or rival, **nemesis**, derived from Nemesis, the Greek goddess of vengeance, means the prospect of receiving retributive justice: 'At last the cruel leader was the peoples' prisoner, awaiting his nemesis alone in his cell.'

nepotism

Nepotism is occasionally confused with the right of sons only, or more specifically the eldest son (primogeniture), to inherit property, positions or other favours. Originally **nepotism** referred to favouritism among relatives, but now it is more widely applied to the practice of handing out advantages to relatives or friends over more deserving candidates.

new

Watch for the unnecessary use of **new**: 'new discovery'; 'new developments'; 'new breakthrough'. You would hardly expect to gain attention by announcing an old discovery, would you?

nicety, niceness

While many writers avoid using **nice** because of its former over-use (it's due for a comeback, surely) we shouldn't shun **nicety** and **niceness**, both of which have useful meanings. A **nicety** is a subtle point of detail; a delicacy of refinement: 'He was a brilliant master of the niceties of English.' **Niceness** is a safe and fresh way of conveying a combination of charm, sympathy, kindliness and modesty.

nominal

See **token, nominal, notional**

none

Contrary to widely held belief **none** can be singular or plural according to the sense in the context. If **none** expresses the singular idea of 'not one' then it is singular: 'All five books are well written but none (i.e. **not one**) has been a bestseller.' But where **none** suggests a multiplicity of 'not any', none is plural: 'We looked for suitable gifts but none were to be found.' In each of these examples your ear would have told you that both 'none have been a bestseller' and 'none was to be found' sound wrong. But you'll also come across cases where despite following the 'rule' the sentences still sound dud. 'None of the gang was caught' and 'None of the patients was really ill' are pedantically correct but in each case the plural **were** instead of the singular **was** would sound better. It's a matter of gingerly feeling your way and making sure that once you proceed with singular or plural the sentence remains consistent.

none the less, nonetheless

Although traditionally written in three words and sometimes hyphenated, **nonetheless** the single word is now generally accepted.

normally, normalcy, normality

Normal once meant 'according to a rule or standard', but for a long while now we have been using **normal** and **normally** to mean usual, common or typical. The *Oxford English Dictionary* dates **normalcy** back to 1857 but its synonym **normality** is now preferred.

notwithstanding

See **pace, according to, notwithstanding**

nought, naught

Nought is the correct spelling for zero (0); **naught**, meaning nothing, is occasionally found in such constructions as 'All their efforts came to naught.' **Naught** means zero in the US.

nubile

It would take a brave or foolish writer to use the original meaning of **nubile** to describe a woman: 'suitable or ready for marriage'. Its now well-established meaning is 'physically and sexually attractive' and is replete with suggestive overtones usually left to the imagination.

nugatory, nuggety

Something **nugatory** is worthless and trivial; someone **nuggety** is stocky and rugged.

nullify, mollify

To **nullify** is to make useless, to cancel out or, indeed, to render null and void. To **mollify** is to appease and soothe.

observance, observation

An **observance** is a ceremony or custom, as is the act of complying with a law or custom: 'The military insisted on strict observance of the curfew.' **Observation** is the act of watching, or noting information: 'He was awarded the medal for his observations on the mating of the rare white seal.'

obtain

See **get, acquire, obtain, secure**

obtuse

See **abstruse, obtuse**

occupied, preoccupied

In the sense of using one's time, being **occupied**
means being busy; being **preoccupied** means
being absorbed, engrossed and oblivious to all
around you.

odd, queer, etc.

Many people today hesitate to use **queer** in its
original meaning of strange and unusual for fear
of being misunderstood. Even an innocent
remark like 'I'm feeling a little queer' is likely
to provoke sniggers and guffaws. Now that the
word has been effectively hijacked to mean
homosexual it's perhaps safer to use alternatives:
**odd, peculiar, curious, unreal, suspicious,
dotty**, etc.

offer

See **proffer, offer**

older, oldest

See **elder, older, eldest, oldest**

one another

See **each other, one another**

onward, onwards

Onward is the adjective: 'Despite the hail of
gunfire the car maintained its onward course.'
Both **onward** and **onwards** are adverbs, with
the latter more in general use: 'The car kept
coming, despite the fierce gunfire, onwards to
the escapees' hideout.'

opposed, opposite
See **diametric**, **opposite**, **opposed**

optimistic, confident, etc.
To be **optimistic** is to look on the bright side of
things, to expect the best in everyone, to believe
that good will triumph over evil, to be always
cheerfully hopeful. You can see that **optimistic**
invites all kinds of interpretation as to its
meaning. But if you wish to convey hope,
confidence, expectancy, encouragement,
certainty or a similar specific meaning you
should consider using more precise adjectives:
hopeful, **confident**, **expectant**, **encouraged**,
certain, etc.

optimum, optimal
Optimum is often mistakenly used to indicate
the most, the greatest, the biggest or the best.
In fact, **optimum** (and its fancy synonym
optimal) means the best result produced by a
set of conflicting factors. The **optimum** selling
price for a newspaper isn't necessarily the
highest or the lowest, but that which will attract
the public to buy it while still making a profit
for the publisher.

orchestrate, organise
In its non-musical sense **orchestrate** does not
mean to **organise**, but to arrange something
for a special or maximum effect.

ordinance, ordnance
An **ordinance** is a regulation or decree;
ordnance means military armament,
munitions and supplies.

oriel, oriole

An **oriel** is a projecting window, usually from an upper storey; the **oriole** is a brightly plumaged songbird.

orotund, rotund

An **orotund** voice is rich and resonant; and **orotund** speech is loud and pompous. **Rotund** can also be applied to speech – meaning sonorous and grandiloquent – but it is mostly used to describe the human figure – plump and round.

outdoor, outdoors

'She loved outdoor activities' (adjective); 'He loved to paint outdoors' (noun).

over, more than

Over is a highly useful catch-all word, and there's the catch: over-use. Some writers object to its use in place of **more than**: 'He weighed in at over fifteen stone'; 'She collected over six hundred Barbie dolls.' The use of **over** in other contexts is also regarded as sloppy: 'The complaint was over the redundancy payments' (should be 'caused by' or 'triggered by'); 'The strike was over increased employment guarantees' (should be 'for' or 'about'); 'She expessed her worries over the missing child' ('about' is better). It's worth taking a little care over **over**.

overt

See **covert, overt**

Pace, according to, notwithstanding

Fowler says forthrightly that this Latinism 'is one
we could very well do without in English'
because it is so widely misunderstood. Faced
with a sentence containing *pace*: 'But in the
House of Lords there is no hilarity – *pace* Lord
Salisbury's speech last night . . .' many people
are prone to think that *pace* means
notwithstanding. Another guess is that it
means according to. *Pace* (pronounced **pay-say**
or **pah-chay**) is a nicety expressing polite
disagreement but with due defence to, and is
thus used to acknowledge the author of a quote:
'The inscription in E. M. Forster's *A Passage to
India*, "God si love" is not, *pace* Andrew
Motion, a typographical mistake that was never
corrected, but an observation noted at Moghul
Sarai railway station and recorded in Forster's
diary for January 1913.'

pacific, Pacific

A **pacific** person is against the use of force and
thus war. **Pacific** relates to the Pacific Ocean,
its islands and adjoining land mass, e.g. the
Pacific Rim.

palpate, palpitate

When a doctor **palpates** he examines by the
sense of touch and pressure. **Palpitate** means
to tremble but it is mostly used to describe an
abnormally fast and uneven heart beat.

panacea

'The team found that common aspirin and several day's rest was the panacea for the latest 'flu epidemic'. **Panacea** is used incorrectly here; a **panacea** is a universal remedy for *all* ills.

parlay, parley

In betting parlance **parlay** means to stake all the winnings from one bet on to the next; to **parley** is to discuss informally with an opponent terms for ceasing hostilities.

parochial

See **provincial, parochial**

parsimony, penury

Parsimony means frugality and stinginess; **penury** means extreme poverty: 'The old man was parsimonious which was why he was never penurious.'

pastiche, parody

Pastiche is sometimes used instead of **parody** but there is a difference. A **pastiche** is a play, painting or some other creation that imitates and borrows styles from other artists and periods. A **parody** is a humorous – intentional or unintentional – or satirical imitation of another's work.

pathos

See **bathos, pathos, bathetic, pathetic**

peaceful, peaceable

Peaceful means tranquil and calm; someone **peaceable** is attracted to peace and tranquillity.

pedlar, pedler, pedaller

Someone who **peddles** or hawks goods from house to house or person to person is a **pedlar** in the UK and a **pedler** in the US. A **pedaller** is usually found riding on a bicycle.

peninsula, peninsular

A **peninsula** (no 'r') is a projecting strip of land while **peninsular** is the adjective, found in Peninsular War and the full name of P&O – The Peninsular & Oriental Company.

penury

See **parsimony, penury**

people, persons

Where the sense of a group needs to be conveyed, or there is an indeterminate number of persons, use **people**: 'Hundreds of people hurled themselves at the turnstiles.' Where a sense of individuality needs to be preserved, **persons** is sometimes appropriate: 'The number of persons injured in the blast is expected to reach double figures.'

percentage, proportion, part

Percentage and **proportion** are habitually used when neither a percentage nor a proportion is remotely involved in the statement: 'A large percentage of the shareholders voted for the changes' (meaning 'many'); 'The biggest proportion of the profits will be ploughed back into research' (meaning 'most'). Where an actual percentage figure or a known proportion is involved, fair enough; otherwise **part** is a more honest word.

permeate, pervade, penetrate

These, together with **saturate** and **impregnate**, are near-synonyms; in usage the differences are fine though recognised. **Permeate** is the action of passing through by diffusion: a gas or smell can permeate a room. **Pervade** means to spread through, gradually and subtly: a sense of fear can pervade a roomful of people. To **penetrate** implies force or at least the overcoming of resistance.

Persecuted unjustly and other pleonasms

A **pleonasm** is a simple idea expressed with more words than is necessary. How many times have you heard 'past history' when everyone knows that all history is in the past? A gift is something given, so what is a 'free gift'? Here are a few pleonasms that lurk in everyday speech and writing:

future prospects	advance warning
actual facts	completely full
small detail	relic of the past
general consensus	join together
universal panacea	usual habits
moment in time	violent explosion
close proximity	original source
interspersed among	revert back
general public	repeat again
new innovations	audible click
downward plunge	final outcome
consensus of opinion	serried rows

persecute, prosecute

To **persecute** is to ill-treat, harass or oppress someone; to **prosecute** is to bring a criminal action against someone. **Prosecute** is sometimes used to mean carrying out a task or undertaking: 'He prosecuted his duties with the utmost vigour.'

personally

Often part of a pleonasm (see p. 109): 'The minister said that he would personally inspect the site himself.' It is difficult to visualise any other way in which the minister could make the inspection. Use only when necessary, as in: 'Although the board had voted against the merger the chairman hinted that he, personally, had misgivings about the decision.'

personify, impersonate

To **personify** is to attribute human characteristics to an abstraction or object: 'He was greed personified.' To **impersonate** is to pretend to be another person, usually by copying that person's appearance and mannerisms.

persons

See **people, persons**

pertinent, pertinacious

Pertinent means relevant; to be **pertinacious** is to be resolute in purpose, stubborn and unyielding.

pervade

See **permeate, pervade, penetrate**

perverse, perverted

To be **perverse** is wilfully to deviate from normal expectations; to be persistently obstinate. To be **perverted** is to deviate from the norm to abnormal, immoral or corrupt behaviour or standards.

pharmacist

See **chemist, druggist, pharmacist**

phase, faze

A **phase** is a state or period in a sequence of events: 'Both her children went through the dreaded "I won't" phase.' Surprisingly it is sometimes confused with **faze**, meaning to disconcert, confuse or worry: 'The fact that his trousers had split didn't faze him one bit.'

pick

See **choose, pick**

picturesque, picaresque

Picturesque means visually pleasing and charming; **picaresque** is an episodic form of fiction featuring the adventures of a rogue hero.

piebald, skewbald

A **piebald** horse has black and white markings; a **skewbald** horse is brown or fawn and white.

platonic, Platonic, plutonic

Platonic (capital 'P') relates to the philosophical teachings of Plato; **platonic** (small 'p') is almost always associated with the term **platonic love**, meaning a love or affection that is spiritual and non-sexual between opposite sexes. **Plutonic** is a geological term that pertains to rocks that have originated from the earth's molten mass.

plebiscite, referendum, poll, ballot, election

A **plebiscite** is a direct vote by citizens on an issue of supreme national importance such as a change in sovereignty or frontier. A **referendum** is usually accepted to mean a direct vote by citizens to ratify a proposed change in the law or constitution. A **poll** is the casting and recording of votes in an **election**, which is a democratic process in which candidates are selected for office. A **ballot** is the practice of electing candidates or deciding upon a course of action by marking the choice on a paper which is deposited in a sealed ballot box and afterwards counted.

Poo, Pooh

At least one newspaper stepped in it when reporting on an auction at Bonhams at which a lump of fossilised dinosaur dung was to be offered for sale. In its report the paper jocularly referred to the item as 'polished pooh'. This occasioned an avalanche of complaint mail of which this letter is typical: 'Bonhams is not auctioning "polished pooh" but polished **poo**. By failing to maintain this important distinction, well-loved phrases such as "Wherever I go there's always Pooh", come to take an unfortunate meaning which Pooh-lovers like myself find odious.'

---

point of view
See **standpoint, point of view, viewpoint**

policy
See **ambition vs policy**

populist, popularist, populariser
Populist derives from the nineteenth-century US People's Party and is still sometimes used to describe a politician on the side of the 'little man'. A **populariser** is someone who makes causes attractive and acceptable to the public. **Popularist** is occasionally incorrectly used for **populariser** but as a word it was pensioned off a century ago.

portentous
See **pretentious, portentous**

position
See **situation, position**

pragmatic, practical
A **pragmatic** person approaches a problem with practical considerations and results in mind rather than with theories. Even so, the pragmatic approach is not necessarily practical. A **practical** person is also not too impressed by theory but knows how to do things and actually gets them done.

prawn
See **scampi, shrimp, prawn**

précis, résumé
A **précis** (with or without the accent) is a written

summary of the essential points of a text or speech; a **résumé** (with the accents) is a descriptive summary, usually of some event. A **resume** in the US is a *CV* or *curriculum vitae* in the UK.

precipitate, precipitant, precipitous

All three derive from the Latin *praecipitare* (to throw down headlong), and all are concerned with unexpected and hasty action. 'She precipitated her dismissal by swearing at the supervisor'; 'You could say that Dawn's swearing at the supervisor was a rather precipitant action.' Some writers object to the use of **precipitous** in this context on the grounds that it means extremely steep (which it also does) but there seems little basis for this view.

Precooked and other prefixes

On offer at most supermarkets are **precooked** meals. But can anything be **precooked**? It is either cooked or it isn't. Perhaps such meals should be **pre-tested** – but just how do you accomplish that? Is a **pre-test** a test before a test? How about a **pre-planned** wedding – no doubt for a couple who are **pre-engaged**? These are redundancies or nonsenses, take your pick. Yet **pre-empt** and **pre-emptive** are perfectly respectable (from the Latin *praeemere*, to buy beforehand), the desirable status eventually won by **precondition**. But when does a condition become a precondition – or do we really mean **prerequisite**?

---

preoccupied

See **occupied, preoccupied**

prescribe, ascribe

Prescribe means to recommend; **ascribe** means to attribute: 'The scientists ascribed the unsettled weather to volcanic activity in the Pacific region.'

presently

See **soon, presently**

pressured, pressurised

'He told the court that he had been constantly pressurised not to give evidence.' This is very loose usage of a scientific term concerned with the compression of gas or liquid. **Pressured** is to be preferred.

presumptuous, presumptive

These are often confused. **Presumptuous** behaviour is bold, insolent, impertinent and overbearing. Something **presumptive** is based on a presumption – the probability that something is or will be true. Prince Charles is the heir presumptive to the Throne.

pretentious, portentous

A **pretentious** person is showy, self-important and pompous and inclined to make exaggerated claims. One meaning of **portentous** is also self-important and pompous, but its primary meaning is: ominously foreshadowing some significant or momentous event.

prevaricate, procrastinate

To **prevaricate** is to act falsely or evasively with

the intention of deceiving; to **procrastinate** is
never to do something today that you can do
tomorrow.

prima facie

See **a priori**, **prima facie**

primate, primate

An ape is a **primate**, which is defined as a
placental animal with flexible hands and feet,
good eyesight and, animal-wise, a highly
developed brain. A **primate** is also an Anglican
Archbishop. Confusion reigned recently at the
Wisconsin Regional Primate Centre which,
when compiling an International Directory of
Primatology, wrote to the Archbishop of
Canada, the Most Rev. Michael Peers,
requesting details of his reproductive status, sex
ratio and age structure. Eventually, you will be
pleased to know, apologies were made all round.

prior, prior to, before

In 'I have a prior engagement' **prior** is used in
its proper adjectival sense, meaning previous.
Some writers, however, are prone to using the
legal **prior to**: 'Prior to the meeting we had a
few drinks.' Hardly admissable when **before** is
available.

prise, pry, prize

To **prise** is to force something open, usually by
levering; figuratively, information can be **prised**
from someone. Although an alternative spelling
is **prize** its use only confuses it with the long
established meaning of **prize**: the reward or
honour given for success or for winning
something. The American usage of **pry open** for

prise is creeping in and, again, is being confused with the traditional meaning of **pry** which is to snoop and meddle or poke your nose into someone else's affairs.

pristine

Often misused to mean spotlessly clean, **pristine** in fact means pure and uncorrupted, original and unspoiled: 'The experts had restored the ancient lamp to its pristine state.' See also **catachrestically speaking**. . .

procrastinate

See **prevaricate, procrastinate**

prodigal, generous

To be **generous** is to be unselfish and ready to give freely; to be **prodigal** is to be recklessly wasteful or extravagant.

product

Product – not **the product**, or **products** – is used increasingly in a catch-all fashion. A film industry spokesman might remark of Britain's failure to make more movies: 'Today there's very little worthwhile product coming out Britain.' Used this way **product** is jargon.

proffer, offer

What little distinction there was or is between the two is exceedingly fine. **Proffer** is more formal and implies offering or tendering in expectation of acceptance.

Problems with prepositions?

Are you **angry with** Simon, or **angry at** Simon?
Do you **cater for** Julie's whims, or **cater to**
them? Have you ever been **compared to** a
famous person, or **compared with** one? Using
prepositions is a bit of a mating game, often
idiomatic, sometimes illogical, and a constant
curse for virtually every writer.

Problematical prepositions fall into groups. In
some cases a certain preposition is prescribed:
'Tom was oblivious of the din', not **oblivious to**.
Then you find that half the population is using
the forbidden preposition anyway. In other cases
different prepositions will supply different
meanings: 'June agreed with the proposal'; 'June
agreed to the proposal'. There are instances
where there is a choice: **affinity with** and
affinity between. Finally, there are
prepositions which aren't needed at all: **visited
with** and **infringe upon** are two common
redundancies.

Here are some of the prepositional matings that
seem to cause confusion:

acquiesce **in**
affinity **with/between** (not **to** or **for**)
agree **to** (accept); agree **with** (concur)
alternative **to**
apropos **of**, or apropos (no preposition)
ask **of/for**
averse **to**
brood **on/over** (not about)
capacity **to/for**

cater **for** (American English is cater **to**)

compare **to** (liken to); compare **with** (to look for differences and similarities)

concur **in** (an opinion); concur **with** (someone)

conform **to/with**

connive **at** (illegal action); connive **with** (a person)

consequent **on**

die **of** (not die **from**)

differ **from** (be unlike); differ **with** (disagree with)

different **from** (preferred to different **to**, and also to the accepted US usage, different **than**)

disgusted **at** (something); disgusted **with** (someone)

encroach (no preposition but usually followed by **on/upon**)

identical **to** (not **with**)

inferior/superior **to** (not **than**)

knack **of**

meet **with** (problems, delays); meet people (not meet **with** – preposition not needed)

oblivious **to/of**

opposite **to** (not **from**)

partake **of**

participate **in**

privilege **of**

substitute **for** (not **with**)

sympathetic **to**

sympathy **for** (having compassion for another); sympathy **with** (sharing feelings with another)

program, programme

For general usage **programme** is traditional in the UK; **program**, though, is the norm in computer language.

propensity, proclivity

Both mean a natural tendency or inclination although **proclivity** is sometimes given a twist to imply 'unnatural', as in: 'We all knew about Heather's sexual proclivities.'

prophecy, prophesy

Prophecy is the noun; **prophesy** is the verb: 'The old man prophesied a hard winter, but his last prophecy had been totally wrong.'

proportion

See **percentage, proportion, part**

prosecute

See **persecute, prosecute**

protagonist, antagonist

'Mr Castle-Reeves is fortunate to have two talented protagonists to help him in the forthcoming by-election.' The use of **protagonist** to mean ally or supporter is a common error; a **protagonist** is the leading character or key player in an event, and thus there can never be more than one. An **antagonist** is an adversary or opponent.

protest, protest against

Many grammarians object to the use of **protest at**, **protest against** and **protest about**: 'The students angrily protested against the closing of the cafeteria.' It is customary to use **protest** alone as a verb as in 'She protested her innocence' but in parallel examples such as, 'The nurses protested the government's rejection of their pay claim' it cries out, as Fowler puts it, for the insertion of **against**.

prosthesis, prothesis

A **prosthesis** is an artificial or mechanical replacement of a damaged or missing part of the body; **prothesis** is an extra sound placed at the beginning of a word as in the Spanish *escriber* (to write) from the Latin *scribere*.

proverbial

'Always arriving or departing, George was like the proverbial rolling stone.' Because **proverbial** here points to a proverb (A rolling stone gathers no moss) it is used correctly; quite commonly, however, it is used when there is no connection with a proverb at all.

provided that, providing that

Usage favours **provided that** but there is little to choose between them.

provincial, parochial

In the UK **provincial** tends to apply to anything outside London; strictly speaking it means relating to the provinces. The term is often used (by city dwellers) in a derogatory way: 'Her taste in theatre, my dear, is somewhat provincial.' The compass of **parochial** shrinks to parish boundaries; it also implies a viewpoint that's narrow and limited in outlook and interest.

pry

See **prise, pry, prize**

punctilious

See **meticulous, punctilious, conscientious, thorough**

purposely, purposefully

Purposely means intentionally, on purpose: 'He purposely tripped me.' **Purposefully** means determined or resolute: 'She took a deep breath and purposefully rose to address the meeting.'

pursuant to, pursuivant

Pursuant to means in accordance or agreement with: 'Pursuant to regulations, passengers must disembark from the port side.' The word is now a bit old-fashioned and legalistic. **Pursuivant** is an heraldic term.

qua

The occasional appearance of this Latin word understandably rattles many people. It acts as a sort of abbreviation and means 'by virtue of being' or 'in the capacity of' or 'in the role of': 'Emma sought his opinion, not qua her legal adviser but as a friend, on the question of proceeding.' In most cases **as** is an excellent plain substitute.

queer

See **odd, queer, etc**.

question, begging the

To **beg the question** is to assume the truth of a proposition that remains to be proved. A secondary meaning, not unknown in politics, is avoiding an answer by posing another question.

quietness, quietude, quiescent

Quietness and **quietude** are synonyms describing a state of little or no sound or movement. **Quietude**, however, is commonly used to describe a state of peace and tranquillity: 'During her convalescence, Sarah enjoyed the quietude of their Cornwall retreat.' **Quiescent**, the adjective, can also mean **quiet** but its main use is to indicate a state of inactivity or dormancy.

quixotic

Often misused to mean foolishly pointless, it really means to be hopelessly idealistic and ridiculously chivalrous.

quote, cite

Both overlap in their meaning of referring to or reciting something said or written: 'To support her argument she quoted/cited several authoritative opinions on the subject.' **Cite** is also used to mean 'mention or commend', usually for bravery: 'During the Vietnam War he was cited on three occasions.'

rack

See **wrack, rack**

racialism, racism

Although the two have in the past been allotted separate meanings – the *Routledge Dictionary of Race and Ethnic Relations* has **racism** = discriminatory attitudes and beliefs; **racialism** = abuse directed at another race – both are now viewed as synonyms, with the shorter **racism** being preferred.

racket, racquet

The Times prescribes **racket** for tennis, for noise and commotion, and for fraudulent enterprise. **Racquet** is an acceptable alternative spelling for the tennis racket.

range

See **spectrum, range**

rapt

See **wrapped, rapt**

ravaged, ravenous, ravished, ravishing

Ravaged means extensively damaged, ruined or destroyed, although the word is often used romantically: 'She was swept away by his sunburned, ravaged face.' To be **ravenous** is to be famished, starving. **Ravish** requires some care in usage; its primary meaning is to enrapture, to be carried away with great delight, but in usage it is now so associated with rape and violation that ambiguity is likely. **Ravishing** is safe; it means enchanting, delightful, lovely.

recount, re-count

To **recount** is to relate or recite the details of a story or event; to **re-count** is to count again.

recover, re-cover

To **recover** is to regain or retrieve something after losing it: 'She quickly recovered her senses.' To **re-cover** something is to cover again: 'They had the suite re-covered in dark red velvet.'

reduce

See **exhaust, deplete, reduce**

referee

See **umpire, referee**

referendum

See **plebiscite, referendum, poll, ballot, election**

regard for, regard to

To have **regard for** someone is to respect and admire that person: 'He always held the highest regard for her.' The phrases **in regard to** and **as regards** mean regarding or concerning: 'In regard to the matter you raised yesterday, it is being dealt with.' Both are a bit stiff and pompous.

regardless, irregardless

Although you hear it from time to time, **irregardless** doesn't exist. **Regardless** is used in two senses: as an adjective to mean unthinking and reckless ('The two men fought on the balcony, regardless of the six-storey drop') and as an adverb meaning in spite of everything: 'Its rudder damaged, spinnaker gone and sails in shreds, the yacht sailed on regardless.'

register, registry

A **register** can be a record of names, transactions, events, correspondence, data, etc.; a **registry** is the place where registers are kept.

registrar, bursar, bursary

A **registrar** keeps registers and official records; a **bursar** manages the financial affairs of a school, college or university. A **bursary** is a scholarship awarded by a school or college.

Reparation, restitution and retribution

Among the many letters received from readers of the first *Word Check* were requests for rulings on usages not covered in the book. Typical was one from Gwasanaeth Prawf Gogledd Cymru (North Wales Probation Service) which is responsible for preparing pre-sentence reports to assist the Court in determining appropriate sentences for offenders: 'The problem is in the use of the words **retribution**, **restitution** and **reparation**. When it is felt that an offender should receive a sentence of community service, which means carrying out unpaid work for the community against which he/she has offended, the expressions used in reports recommending such a sentence include "he should make **retribution/restitution/reparation** to the community he/she has offended". There is a view here that **retribution** in this context is incorrect but this view is not universally shared.'

reiterate, iterate

If **reiterate** means, as it does, to repeat, or say again, is **iterate** its opposite? No, it means exactly the same, so there's little point in using the lesser known synonym.

relation, relative

In the context of kinship the two are synonyms; take your choice.

Word Check offered the following:

Reparation is the act of making amends, or redressing a wrong, of repairing or restoring some injury or damage. **Restitution** can have an identical meaning, but it also has recognition in law as the act of compensating for loss or injury, especially by returning something to its original state – for example, the removal of graffiti by the perpetrator. The meaning of **retribution** carries with it overtones of punishment and revenge (the word is from the Latin *retribuere* which means 'to repay') and Divine judgment and should only be used to mean the act of punishing or taking vengeance for some sin or injury.

You will gather from the above that the preferred word in the context of usage by the Probation Service ought to be **restitution**.

renascence, renascent, renaissance, Renaissance

Renascence is an alternative spelling of **renaissance**, meaning a revival or rebirth, usually in the context of culture or learning. **Renascent** is more often used than **renascence**, and means growing and becoming active again. **The Renaissance** (with a capital 'R') is the period, from the fourteenth to the sixteenth century, marking the European revival of art and classical scholarship, the end of the Middle Ages and the rise of the modern world.

repel, repulse

Although both **repel** and **repulse** mean 'to force or drive back' they have other meanings, the usage of which can be confusing. The related word **repulsive**, for example, means causing distaste and disgust, but we do not say 'His filthy, drunken state repulsed the other passengers'; instead we use **repelled**. Nor is **repel** appropriate when the meaning is to drive away or reject; here the usage demands **repulse**: 'She repulsed his proposal by throwing the flowers at him and slamming the door.'

repository

See **depository, repository**

requisite, requirement

In the sense of something needed, essential or indispensible, both are synonyms. But **requirement** also means an obligation or something demanded: 'One of the requirements for the job was absolute punctuality.' **Requisite** is also an adjective: 'She had the requisite qualifications for the job.'

responsible

See **accountable, responsible**

resin, rosin

These should not be regarded as alternative spellings although they usually are. **Resin** is a gummy exudation from trees or plants (amber, copal) but the word is also now applied to a wide range of synthetic plastics. **Rosin** is the residue from the distillation of turpentine used in varnishes and paints.

resister, resistor

A **resister** is one who resists; a **resistor** is a component that introduces resistance into an electrical circuit.

résumé

See **précis, résumé**

rigour, rigorous, rigor

Rigour is a state of strictness, inflexibility, severity or hardship; **rigorous** is the adjective: 'The monks were subjected to three years of rigorous discipline.' **Rigor** is the medical condition of muscular rigidity, hence *rigor mortis*.

riposte, retort

A **riposte** is a quick, sharp reply. **Retort** means the same but it is usually reserved to indicate a stronger, sometimes angry, sometimes sarcastic reply.

rocks, stones

Boys throw **stones** in Britain; in the US they throw **rocks** and this usage, via films and TV, is creeping into the UK. The separate words are worth preserving.

rotund

See **orotund, rotund**

round, around, about

'She looked round' or 'She looked around'? In the unintentionally comic first example, there is a temptation to substitute **around**, but this would be a departure from British usage (**around** is preferred in the US). A certain flexibility is obviously called for but some usages

have stuck: 'We waited around'; 'We drove
around'; 'The smell lingered around the house';
'All year round'; 'Fenced all round'; 'The wheels
turned round'; 'The boxer gradually came round'
are just a few. **Around** is also increasingly used
to mean 'approximately': 'We've had around
fifty replies.' **About** is to be preferred.

rouse, arouse

Both mean to awaken or stir out of inactivity,
but **rouse** tends to imply a physical response
('He roused the men from their bunks') while
arouse suggests a more emotional reaction:
'Sally's frequent disappearances began to arouse
his suspicions.'

rout, route

A **rout** is a disorderly retreat; an overwhelming
defeat; **to rout** is to cause a defeat or retreat.
Rout also means to dig over or rummage. A
route is the course planned or taken from one
place to another during a journey. Watch the
spelling of **routeing**: 'Fred was in charge of
routeing the buses.'

rustic, rusticate

Something **rustic** is associated with the country
or rural life, supposedly simple and
unsophisticated. To **rusticate** is to banish to the
country but its most common usage is to be
sent down from a university as a punishment.

sanguine, sanguinary

A frustrating pair. **Sanguinary** has one bloody
meaning: attended with much bloodshed,
bloodthirsty, flowing or stained with blood.
Sanguine also has its bloody aspect; it means
blood-red and ruddy. But it also means

optimistic, cheerful and confident. Use both with care.

sauce
See **ketchup, sauce, chutney, pickle**

scampi, shrimp, prawn
Scampi are prawns usually fried in breadcrumbs or batter. **Prawns**, probably *Pandalus borealis* or *Palaemon penaeus*, are the crustaceans that grace prawn cocktails. **Shrimp** are a large family of marine decapods of which the *Crangon vulgaris* is the main edible member.

scare, scarify
To **scare** is to frighten; to **scarify** is to scratch, abrade, break up or wound.

sceptic, septic
A **sceptic** is a doubter who is unwilling to believe anything without ample proof. Something **septic** causes infection or putrefaction; in a **septic tank** sewage is broken down by bacteria.

scotch
To **scotch** a rumour is to suppress it. Plans can be **scotched**, too, when it means 'to put an end to'. **Scotch** in these contexts is not a slang term but a word, deriving from the Old French *escocher*, 'to cut'.

scrimp, skimp
Both mean to be sparing, frugal, stingy: 'Their mother scrimps/skimps on food but smokes like a chimney and drinks like a fish.' **Skimp** has a second meaning which is to do something carelessly, hastily and in a slapdash manner.

scull, skull

Scull can be a single oar, a long, narrow racing boat, or the action of pulling on one or a pair of oars. The **skull** is the bony skeleton of the head.

scuttle, scupper

These are not strictly interchangeable. A **scupper** is an opening on the deck or side of a ship for draining off water. A **scuttle** is also an opening but it is a covered hatchway for access. If such openings are made below the waterline the ship can be **scuttled,** or sunk. **Scuttle** but more usually **scupper** are both used to mean to wreck or ruin: 'The arrival of half a dozen ice-cream vans scuppered Bert's plans to make a killing.'

seasonal, seasonable

Seasonal means occurring at a certain season, as in 'seasonal storms' and 'seasonal labour'. **Seasonable** means 'suitable to' or 'in keeping with the season'.

secure

See **get, acquire, obtain, secure**

sew

See **sow, sew**

shear, sheer

Shear means to cut off (hair), break off (metal, etc.), or strip off (powers, privileges, etc.). **Sheer** can mean fine and transparent (stockings, silk), steep (road, cliff) or absolute ('She laughed for sheer joy'). **Sheer** also means to deviate or swerve but in this sense **veer** appears to be the more popular choice.

Sex and gender

Sex was once universally used to mean the differences beteen male and female; since then usage of the word has widened enormously and one usage in particular – 'They claimed they had sex five times a week' – to mean sexual intercourse, has virtually levered the word away from its primary meaning. Because of the biological connotations of **sex** (the word) many writers and feminists in particular have nominated **gender** as its substitute to mean the difference between being male and masculine and being female and feminine. **Gender** covers the social functions, status and expectations of males and females: **gender roles** instead of **sex roles** and **gender gap** instead of **sex gap** are now standard terms. There exists also a quest for **gender-fair language** (men and women, lawyer, dentist) and **gender-free language** (student is okay; chambermaid, clergyman and businessman aren't). There is, however, still plenty of scope for **sex**: **sex appeal**, **sex shop**, **sex-starved**, **sexploitation**, **sex change** but definitely not **sexpot** which, claim feminists, narrows the woman's entire personhood to her sexuality and woman-as-tempter stereotype.

shibboleth

Shibboleth is misused variously to mean an entrenched custom, an old saying or a sacred belief. It was in fact the old Hebrew word for an ear of corn and was used as a password by the Gileadite tribe to identify their enemies, the Ephraimites. 'Say shibboleth,' they demanded.

If the reply was 'sibboleth' another Ephraimite bit the dust – 42,000 in all. So today a **shibboleth** is a catchphrase, test or custom that reliably distinguishes the members of a group or social class from another.

Shi'ite, Shia

The two main groups of Muslims are the **Shia** (preferred to **Shi'ite**) Muslims and the **Sunni** Muslims.

shortage, shortfall

A **shortage** is an insufficient amount or a deficiency; a **shortfall** is the failure to meet some requirement or target and the extent of it: 'The fundraising goal suffered a shortfall of some £15,000.'

shrimp

See **scampi, shrimp, prawn**

sick, sickly, ill

To **be sick** is a euphemism for **to vomit**, so **ill** is increasingly substituted for **sick** to mean a state of sickness or being unwell – the usage is about evenly divided. An **ill/sick** Australian resolves the dilemma by saying, 'I'm crook'. Someone **sickly** is unhealthy, weak, and disposed to frequent ailments.

silly

See **crass, silly, stupid, gross**

simple, simplistic

The two are not synonyms. **Simplistic**, although over-used, means excessively simplified to the point of naïvety. The difference is made clear here: 'Dalton's deductions were brilliantly simple, while the solution put forward by Keene was just too simplistic.'

situation, position

More often than not **situation** is used as a bloat word to inflate the importance of a statement: 'It was a typical confrontational situation' for 'it was a typical confrontation' is a fair example. But with overuse toppling **situation** from fashion, its cousin **position** seems to be taking over: 'The position in regard to the need to increase railway fares is that it is being kept under review.' This is gobbledegook which, when translated, could mean, 'The possibility of increasing railway fares is being considered.'

skewbald
See **piebald, skewbald**

skull
See **scull, skull**

slang
See **The joys of jargon, slang, colloquialism, vernacular, argot, cant, lingua franca and gobbledegook**

sodality, solidarity, solidity
Solidarity expresses a unity of interests, opinions, feelings and responsibilities that binds members of a class or community. **Solidity** is the state of being solid. **Sodality**, a rather less common word, is a fellowship or fraternity.

sometime, some time, sometimes
Some time and to a lesser extent **sometime** are used to indicate 'at some time or other': 'The Smiths moved away some time ago.' Fowler makes the valid point that **sometime** should be reserved for its adjectival sense meaning former: 'The sometime president of the Board of Trade.' **Sometimes** means occasionally, now and then.

somewhere, someplace
The traditional and perfectly adequate **somewhere** is standing up rather well to the American import **someplace**.

soon, presently
Although the original meaning of **presently** (immediately) was supposed to have become obsolete a couple of centuries ago it is still very

much in evidence. This causes immense confusion with the contemporary meaning of **presently**, which is soon, in a while. Curiously, the old meaning never died out in Scotland, so the Scots win points for consistency. If you wish to avoid ambiguity you'll use **soon, now, currently, shortly,** etc. See also **directly.**

sort of
See **kind of, sort of**

Soul, sole

Kielder Ferries must not only be a profitable business but a most celestial one, ferrying **souls** from one heavenly bank to the other. All Kielder Water needs is a new name befitting its paradisiacal role. How about Holy Water?

From the *Newcastle Journal*

---

sow, sew

You **sew** with needle and thread (sewed, sewn) and **sow** seeds (sowed, sown). A **sow** (pronounced as rhyming with **how**) is also a female pig.

spasmodic, sporadic

These are near synonyms but **spasmodic** means happening in short, irregular and unexpected bursts or spasms, while something **sporadic** occurs intermittently, at scattered intervals: 'The thunder continued sporadically throughout the afternoon.'

spectrum, range

Spectrum is often used instead of **range**. Use **range**.

spokesman, spokeswoman, spokesperson

In the view of *The Times*, all of these are 'ugly' words. Avoid them and the evil blight of political correctness by using more specific words: source, official, representative, aide, etc.

stalactite, stalagmite

A **stalactite** (*c* for ceiling) hangs down; a **stalagmite** (*g* for ground) projects up.

stanch, staunch

As the verb meaning to stem the flow of blood, **stanch** is preferred, leaving **staunch** as an adjective meaning firmly loyal and steadfast.

standpoint, point of view, viewpoint

Some object to **standpoint** but it is a respectable word, deriving from the German *standpunkt*, meaning a position from which something is

viewed, usually mental rather than physical.
Point of view and **viewpoint** mean the same.

stolid, solid

Stolid means dull, impassive and showing little
feeling or perception; it is often applied in a
derogatory sense to indicate stupidity. **Solid,**
used in the same context, means dependable –
a real brick.

stones

See **rocks, stones**

storey, story

A **storey** is a floor in a building; a **story** is a
tale.

straight, strait

Extensions to these words require care: **straight**
and narrow (although **strait** and narrow in the
Bible), **straightedge, straight-faced,**
straightforward; dire **straits, strait-laced,**
straitjacket, straitened circumstances. It is a
good idea to use a dictionary as a guide.

stupid

See **crass, silly, stupid, gross**

style, stile

A **stile** is the set of wooden steps to help you
climb over a fence.

succeed, follow

Often regarded as synonyms but they're not. To
follow means to go or come after and in the
same direction; to **succeed**, in this context,
means to come next in order or sequence:

'When the old moose died they wondered who would succeed as the head of the herd.'

summoned, summonsed

You can be **summoned** to appear, for example, at a hearing or a court. If, however, you are presented with a **summons** you are therefore **summonsed**.

suit, suite

Although pronounced differently, confusion is not unknown: a **suit** of clothes but a **suite** of furniture; strong **suit**, follow **suit**; a **suit** of cards; a **law-suit**; but a presidential **suite** (of rooms), a musical **suite**, a **suite** of attendants.

supersede, surpass

Supersede means to supplant or replace with something or someone superior to the original. To **surpass** is to be better or greater than or superior in excellence or achievement: 'Her results at the last Olympics surpassed even her own records.'

superficial, cosmetic

'We've made some changes but they're only cosmetic' is a usage very much in vogue. **Superficial** is more to the point and preferred.

surge

See **upsurge, surge**

surrounded

Surrounded means encircled or enclosed, so phases like 'completely surrounded' and 'surrounded on three sides' are incorrect.

Sweater, jersey, jumper, pullover, etc.

In matters of mercery, usage departs from often vague or out-dated dictionary definitions, so it's difficult to describe precisely what a jumper is, or a sweater, or any similar upper garment. Here's a cross-section of opinion.

A **sweater** is knitted, neither tight nor loose, and is a synonym for **jumper**; the latter term being used more to describe a child's garment. A **jersey** or **guernsey** was originally a heavy woollen sweater and although *de rigueur* in Scotland and among sportsmen the word, if not the garment, seems to be falling from use. A **pullover** can be with or without sleeves and is loose enough to slip easily over the head; it tends to be a male garment. That notable eponym the **cardigan** is distinguished by having buttons up the front; in a **twinset** it is worn over a matching short-sleeved sweater. A **T-shirt** is usually short-sleeved, usually of cotton and takes its name from its shape. A **tank-top**, extremely fashionable a decade or two ago, is a sleeveless, lightweight, upper garment with wide shoulder straps. The trade or generic term for all of the above is simply **tops**.

swop, swap

Meaning to exchange, **swap** is universal and preferred; **swop** is a purely English variant.

swot, swat

These are two different words. To **swot** is to study or cram for an examination; to **swat** is to smack or hit sharply: 'We did little all day but swat flies and mosquitoes.'

syndrome, synergy, symbiosis

Each of these is about relationships. A **syndrome** is a combination of symptoms and signs that suggests some disease or disorder. **Synergy** is now popularly used to mean 'productive relationship' or 'mutually beneficial relationship' but what it really means is the action of two groups or substances that when combined produce an effect of which each is incapable alone. **Symbiosis** is a biological term defining the interdependency of two animal or plant species.

tautology

Tautology, pleonasm, redundancy and prolixity all belong to the same family that needs more words than necessary to say something. A **tautology** is where the same thing is said twice: 'I'll be leaving at 7 a.m. in the morning'; 'It's a rather puzzling mystery'; 'disastrous tragedy'. See **Persecuted unjustly and other pleonasms**.

temporal, temporary

Temporal relates to real life, to the secular as opposed to the spiritual, to earthly time rather than to eternity. **Temporary** means impermanent, lasting for a short time only.

Don't get out of line when using tandem

Tandem, observed Philip Howard in *The Times*, is a word that is being eroded 'by slipshod extension, which Fowler defined, in his elitist way, as occurring when some accident gives currency among the uneducated to words of learned origin'.

Howard quoted some lapses from his own newspaper: 'Polaris and Trident will run in tandem for a short time'; 'A Germany working in tandem with its partners could play a lead in this rewarding democratic reform'; and a caption to a photo of two hang-gliders, hanging on side-by-side, asserting that they were in tandem when, visibly, they were not.

Tandem, from a pun on the Latin **tandem** meaning at last, in the end, at length, is intended to mean one behind the other, as with a tandem bicycle. This meaning is worth preserving because, as Howard points out, there are plenty of words to mean side-by-side, but only one to mean in line ahead.

tendency, trend

A **tendency** is an inclination, a leaning, a disposition towards something: 'When he'd had a few too many, George had a tendency to fall asleep.' A **trend** is a general movement: 'The current trend is for people to book holidays early.'

tenterhooks

There are no such things as 'tender hooks' and the same applies to 'tenderhooks'. 'She's on tenterhooks waiting for the exam results' means she's in an agony of suspense waiting for the outcome.

that

That is a word we're abandoning. That very sentence is a good example; grammatically and pedantically it should have been written: 'That is a word that we are abandoning.' Whether used as a conjunction or as a relative pronoun, we're dumping **that** wholesale. The general view on this is that when the meaning is clear, **that** can be dropped: 'Are you pleased (**that**) I bought it?'; 'I know (**that**) she'll come tomorrow'; 'Don't you think (**that**) it's a great car?' – all three statements are unambiguous with that omitted. But don't get carried away. 'Mr Benton said yesterday some shares dropped as much as 20%' could mean two things: did Mr Benton make the statement yesterday ('Mr Benton said yesterday that some shares dropped as much as 20%') or did the shares drop yesterday? ('Mr Benton said that yesterday some shares dropped as much as 20%'). When in doubt, retain **that**.

their, they

The use of plural pronouns like **their** and **they** in a singular sense is one of grammar's most slippery slopes. Faced with a 'his and her' couple, or uncertain as to the gender of the antecedent, we're more or less forced to use constructions like 'Nobody will stop us, will they?'; 'Anyone can do as they please'; 'Has anybody not yet completed their exercises?' All three combine a singular antecedent (**nobody, anyone, anybody**) with a plural pronoun and all are considered acceptable except perhaps by pedants. Grammatical alternatives are clumsy: 'Anyone can do as he or she pleases'; or impossible: 'Nobody will stop us, will he or she?'.

think
See **feel, think**

thorough
See **meticulous, punctilious, conscientious, thorough**

thrilled, enthralled
To be **thrilled** is to experience tingling excitement, an intense wave of emotion; to be **enthralled** (held in **thrall**) is to be captivated, spellbound, in a state of fascinated attention.

tight, tightly
Sometimes interchangeable: 'He held her tight/tightly.' But while **tight** suggests a result ('The cork was jammed tight'), **tightly** implies action ('He held him tightly around the neck').

timidity, temerity
Timidity is the tendency to be easily frightened, shy and fearful. **Temerity** means almost the opposite: foolish, reckless boldness.

tirade
See **harangue, tirade**

toilet
See **lavatory**, **toilet**

token, nominal, notional

All three are frequently misused to mean **minimal**. In the sense of 'symbolic gesture' **token** and **nominal** are closely related: a nominal payment and a token payment, meaning partial payment, are the same thing. **Token** also means slight or of no real account: 'The Party regarded his contribution of £200 as merely token support.' **Nominal** means 'not in fact; in name only'; a nominal charge is one removed from reality in that it is small compared to its real value. Something **notional** relates to concepts and hypotheses rather than reality: 'The engineers' notional cost for a single unit was thought to be in the region of £150.'

Teeth and toothsome

In the *New York Times* recently the American wordsmith William Safire railed against the misuse of the word **toothsome**. His target was *Newsweek* which had referred to a model as 'blond and toothsome', clearly intending this to mean that the young lady had a set of outstanding choppers. Even Norman Mailer, writing in *Time* magazine, fell into the **toothsome** trap, using it to mean **toothy**. 'Let's fight cavities,' quipped Safire, 'but stop the decay of a good word.' **Toothsome** means attractive, alluring, delicious or appetising depending upon what you're describing; it does not mean 'toothy' any more than fulsome means 'full'.

total

This has become an immensely popular word, tending to be used in preference to the often more appropriate 'complete', 'whole', 'entire', etc. It is also used when not needed: 'The gate receipts reached a total of £14,647', when obviously £14,657 is the **total**; and 'This game is going to end in total annihilation for West Ham' (football commentator) when annihilation means to completely defeat or destroy. However, it is hard to carp at one new and imaginative use of the word: 'The garage told him the thieves had **totalled** his car.'

toward, towards

Towards is preferred in Britain: 'The baby crawled towards the door.'

toxin, tocsin

Toxin is poison caused by bacteria; a **tocsin** is a bell rung to raise an alarm.

trait, character

Character – of a person, object or group – is the combination of qualities that distinguishes them: 'He was rather a weak character'; 'It was not in the girl's character to be aggressive'. A **trait** is some aspect or feature of a person or that person's behaviour: 'One of auntie's most endearing traits was her boundless optimism.'

transpire, happen, occur

Transpire does not mean **happen** or **occur** but to become known or come to light: 'It transpired that, because she had accidentally overheard something, Jean had known about the affair all along.'

trauma

This word has become debilitated by misuse and over-use. Originally restricted to mean extreme pathological or psychological shock severe enough to have long-lasting effects, it has for some time been trivialised; 'I simply couldn't stand the trauma of going for another job interview.' Return **trauma** and **traumatise** to the serious shelf.

trend

See **tendency, trend**

triple, treble

Meaning threefold, both are interchangeable except in the terms **treble chance** (football pools) and **triple jump** (the hop, step and jump event in athletics).

triumphal, triumphant

Triumphal means celebrating a triumph or victory; **triumphant** means victorious or successful, and rejoicing in it: 'The team returned home, tired, drunk and triumphant.'

true facts

See **facts, true facts, factitious**

truism, truth

A **truism** is not something that is merely true. It is a self-evident truth often expressed as a platitude.

T-shirt

See **sweater, jersey, jumper, pullover, etc**.

ultimate limit

'Heather was driven to the ultimate limit of her patience.' **Ultimate limit** means **limit** and is tautological.

umpire, referee

Same meaning but different words for different games: **umpire** for tennis, hockey and baseball; **referee** for football and boxing.

unable

See **incapable, unable**

unaware, unawares

Unaware is the adjective ('He was unaware of the danger'); **unawares** is the adverb ('She was caught unawares').

underlay, underlie

To **underlay** is to place something beneath or to support something beneath – think of carpet **underlay**. To **underlie** means to lie under something or to act as a foundation: 'Deep and complex analysis underlies the champion's every move.'

understand, appreciate, comprehend

'I appreciate the reasons for your refusal.' **Appreciate** is a popular substitute for **understand** but **appreciate** really means grateful. **Comprehend** is a synonym of **understand** but with the inference of 'complete understanding'.

unexceptional, unexceptionable

Something **unexceptional** is normal, ordinary or commonplace; something **unexceptionable** is acceptable and beyond criticism: 'He said the jury's verdict was severe in some respects but generally unexceptionable.'

Unless

There is a growing tendency among journalists and columnists to use **unless** as an extended pregnant pause: 'Some will demand that China's door to the West must be closed if not slammed, because, despite Deng's promise, international contempt has not been replaced by respect. Unless. Unless a great question is finally faced and answered . . .'

Where this usage achieves the stylistic effect without affectation, well and good; otherwise it is pretentious and is best avoided. As is the similar usage of 'And yet. And yet.' which is also cropping up with alarming frequency. See also **What ever and whatever revisited**.

---

unique facsimile

'These Party Masks are faithfully reproduced from bygone days and are unique facsimiles of the Edwardian and Victorian originals.' No, they are not; they are mass produced **copies** of the original. An **original**, if there is only one, is unique, and it is possible to have a **unique facsimile**; sculptors sometimes have a single exact copy cast from their original sculpture. **Unique** means without like or equal, the only one of its kind, and no 'ifs' or 'buts'.

universal

An obituary in the *Arundel and Brighton News* began: ' "Fr. Gerry", as he was universally known in the Reigate and Redhill area . . .' This is a rather suburban translation of the real meaning of **universal** which is typical of the whole of mankind; existing or prevailing everywhere; cosmic. Better choices for Fr. Gerry would have been always, generally, invariably or regularly.

unsatisfied

See **dissatisfied, unsatisfied**

untimely death, instant death

Death is never timely and as far as we know, no matter how agonisingly drawn out the process preceding it, it is always instant. Don't fall for these clichés.

upsurge, surge

To **surge** is to swell, bulge, well up, gush, rush, heave or flow (or in any combination of these) – and not necessarily upwards. **Upsurge** suggests a rising or increasing surge: 'The police attributed the upsurge of violence to the presence of professional rabble-rousers.'

upward, upwards

Upward is an adjective (upward mobility; an upward slope), and while also an adverb the alternative **upwards** is preferred in this role: 'They climbed upwards for what seemed like an eternity.'

use to, used to

The usage of **use to** as a verb is always in the past tense and follows this form:

- Did you **use to** live in Manchester?
- Didn't you **use to** live in Manchester? (negative sense)
- I know you **used to** live in Manchester.
- Didn't you say you **used not to** like living in London? (negative sense)

vacant, vacuous

Vacant means empty or unoccupied; **vacuous** means not only empty but blank, bereft and mindless: 'The stranger unsettled everyone with his vacuous stare.'

Van Gogh, Vincent van Gogh

Dutch names observe the convention that **van** is in lower case when part of the full name (**Vincent van Gogh, Anthony van Dyke**) but capitalised when used only with the surname (**Van Gogh, Van Dyke**).

venal, venial

Venal means corrupt and open to bribery; **venial** means forgiveable or excusable: a **venial sin** is not one that is evil or monstrous as is often supposed, but one that is trivial and readily pardoned.

veracious, voracious

Veracious means habitually truthful and careful with facts; **voracious** means greedy, rapacious, insatiable.

via

It is fairly common to see **via** used like this:
They came from Victoria to Tower Hill via the
Underground.' Purists like to see the use of **via**
restricted to mean 'by way of' and not 'by
means of': 'They travelled on the Underground
to Tower Hill from Victoria via Embankment.'

visible, visual

Visible means capable of being seen; **visual**
relates to anything involving the sense of sight:
visual arts, **visual** aids, **visually** handicapped,
VDU (**visual** display unit of computers), etc.

viz

Viz is short for the adverb *videlicet* which means
namely – so why not simply use namely, or, that
is to say, or, for example?

vocation, avocation

Although these are increasingly used as
synonyms, they are not, and it is worthwhile
preserving the different meanings. A **vocation** is
a person's regular occupation, profession or
trade; an **avocation** is a diversion from a
person's regular employment – a hobby or a
part-time job.

vomit

See **sick, sickly, ill**

von

When the name is in full, use **von** in lower case
(Paul von Hindenburg); where the surname only
is used, omit the **von**.

voodoo, hoodoo

Voodoo is a Caribbean variety of witchcraft; a **hoodoo** is something or someone who brings bad luck.

wagon, waggon

Although **waggon** is seen occasionally, **wagon** is standard.

wait

See **await, wait**

wary, chary

Not much between these although some writers discern a shade of difference – **wary** = watchful and wily; **chary** = cautious, careful and choosy: 'In her old age she became chary of strangers.'

waste, wastage

Waste is wanton, careless or useless squandering of resources, money or time. **Wastage** is accidental or unavoidable loss through evaporation, leakage, wear or decay. The term **natural** wastage is often applied to a workforce which is reduced in size by voluntary resignation, retirement, etc.

way, weigh

When a ship **weighs** anchor it then gets under **way**.

wedding

See **marriage with, marriage to**

What ever and whatever revisited

'What ever is that funny looking thing over there?' and 'Whatever you do, don't miss that play' are two examples of legitimate usage. What gets up the noses of many grammarians is the slothful use of **or whatever** either as an abbreviation of **or whatever it may be** or to mean something like 'and so on and so forth and who cares anyway?' The example given in the first *Word Check* was, 'On Saturdays I usually do some shopping, wash my hair, empty the cat litter, generally slob around and, you know, whatever . . .' This slangy usage is now further expanded to mean 'it may or may not be so'. Here is Daisy Waugh reviewing a restaurant: 'These restaurants seem to have the idea that it's smart to be too much in demand, to keep people hanging about. Whatever. It is true that at nine o'clock last Monday night Quaglino's was packed.' Do we sense a famous antecedent of Daisy's spinning in his grave?

while, a while, awhile, whilst

While is a notoriously ambiguous word. In its sense of 'at the same time' there is no confusion ('You can talk to me while I iron these shirts') but watch out when the meaning is whereas, although or but: 'My wife likes a good laugh while I watch the news'; 'While he sleeps like a log I love to party all night.' **A while** (noun) can be tricky, too. Make sure you indicate whether it is a **long while** or a **short while**: 'We only waited for a while' implies a short time and, 'We waited for quite a while' indicates a longer time, but both are imprecise. **Awhile** is the adverb which means a short while: 'We waited awhile'. **Whilst** is an old fashioned form of while.

white paper, green paper

A **white paper** is a published report that states the Government's policy on legislation that will come before Parliament. A **green paper** sets out proposals for legislation for discussion and comment by interested parties.

whither

See **wither, whither**

whoever, who ever

'Whoever you are, you are not welcome' uses the word in its correct sense of 'no matter who you are'. The two-word version is used when **ever** is used to emphasise: 'Who ever could have done this?' This general rule of usage also applies to **whatever/what ever, whenever/when ever** and **wherever/where ever**.

whose, who's

Whose always relates to possession; it can ask, 'Whose is this book?' or it can act as a relative pronoun: 'That's the man whose car was stolen.' **Who's** is the abbreviation of **who has** or **who is**.

will, would

Will indicates that something is certain to happen; **would** suggests probability. Confusion can arise if the two are mixed in the same sentence: 'The Minister said the road building programme would be discussed by cabinet and will also be subject to review by the appropriate committees.' Here consistency requires **would** throughout. Select either **will** or **would** to express exactly what is meant, and then use consistently in the sentence.

wither, whither

Spelling is the problem here. **Whither** is little used today but means where to; simply remember the 'wh' of **where**. **Wither** means wilt, decay, decline or dry up; **the withers** are situated between a horse's shoulder-blades.

woman drivers

A tetchy point, this. Facing quite a tide of opinion *The Times* advises 'woman doctors, woman teachers, not women . . .' What does the National Association of Schoolmasters/Union of Women Teachers think about that? Or WPCs – Women Police Constables? Logic suggests singular and plural: **woman driver**, **women drivers**; **woman doctor**, **women doctors**, etc.

wont, won't

The contraction of 'will not' is **won't**: 'Tom simply won't do as he's told.' If you omit the apostrophe you have **wont** either as an adjective meaning accustomed ('He was wont to break into song after his fourth pint') or as a noun meaning habit ('After lunch she read, gardened or dozed as was her wont').

wrack, rack

For **wrack** think of **wreck** and you'll always correctly spell the phrase: 'It went to wrack and ruin.' Almost every other instance requires **rack**;

rack your brains, rack of lamb, rack-and-pionion, rack up, nerve-racking, etc.

wrapped, rapt

'She was huddled by the fire, wrapped in thought.' Or **rapt** in thought? Either would be correct in this example, but keep in mind that the sole meaning of **rapt**, a forerunner of rapture, means engrossed, fascinated, spellbound; and that one of the many meanings of **wrapped** is enclosed or completely absorbed in thought. In this context, **rapt** is preferred.

wreath, wraith

A **wreath** is a circular band of flowers offered as a memorial at funerals; a **wraith** is a ghost or apparition.

write, write to

Avoid the American usage of **write**: 'I will write my congressman to protest.' As a word wag observed: 'You may write the Library of Congress but you write to the British Library.'

Yiddish

See **Jewish, Hebrew, Yiddish**

yoghurt, yogurt, yoghourt

All are correct but **yoghurt** is now fairly standard.

you (the reader)

The use of the pronoun 'one' to represent an indefinite person ('One doesn't do that kind of thing') is stylish and elegant but is increasingly regarded as affected. **You** is the democratic substitute which has the additional advantage of informally but directly addressing the reader: 'You simply don't do that kind of thing.' But a caution to writers torn between the two: 'While you may prefer the more formal to the familiar, one should avoid switching from one person to another.'

A Full List of Titles Available from Mandarin in this series

While every effort is made to keep prices low, it is sometimes necessary to increase prices at short notice. Mandarin Paperbacks reserves the right to show new retail prices on covers which may differ from those previously advertised in the text or elsewhere.

The prices shown below were correct at the time of going to press.